We Survive to Thrive!

Life changing stories by breast cancer survivors

Paula Smith Broadnax

UNI Publish Media – UNI Success Solutions, Inc
Atlanta, Georgia

We survive To Thrive
Life changing stories of breast cancer survivors

Copyright © 2014 Paula Smith Broadnax

ISBN-13: 978-0692306222

ISBN-10: 0692306226

Cover Photo designed by ILGeorgiev

Editor: Jackie S. Henderson, MDiv, DMin

T. Vizion Broadnax
UNI Publish Media – UNI SUCCESS SOLUTIONS, INC
Atlanta, Georgia
uni-likesolutions.com/publish

Printed in the United States of America

We Survive to Thrive

CONTENT

CONTENT

ACKNOWLEDGEMENTS

To my phenomenal Contributors for being willing to share a piece of their lives with the world. I have drawn strength from each of you and am grateful that our paths have crossed.

To Dr. Jackie Henderson for her editing skills. Thank you for your love and support of me and my projects.

To my awesome daughter, Vizion Broadnax, for continuing to venture out to learn new skills (most recently... publishing),You have done a great job! Thank you!

To my beloved husband, Tommie Broadnax, for not only being my help mate but for being a sounding board in the wee hours of the night when many of my revelations came.

PURPOSE

Survive:

Continue to live or exist, in spite of danger or hardship.

Synonym: abiding, continuing, dwelling, enduring, existing, living, persisting, residing

Thrive:

1. To prosper; be fortunate or successful. To grow or develop vigorously; flourish

Synonym: Advance, succeed, flourish, bloom, prosper

WE SURVIVE TO THRIVE was written to inspire all who are going through a life challenge to understand that they can make it and that they have the opportunity for even a better life as a result of what might have seemed like a tragedy.
This book addresses those who have been diagnosed with breast cancer. Their stories tell how they have chosen to thrive, or live a prosperous and enriched life.

WE SURVIVE TO THRIVE contains inspirational stories from contributors who were once labeled as a survivor but have been thriving since their diagnoses.

[1] And he shall be like a tree planted by the rivers of water, that bringeth forth his fruit in his season; his leaf also shall not wither; and whatsoever he doeth shall prosper.

Psalm 1:3 (KJV)

But as for you, ye thought evil against me; but God meant it unto good, to bring to pass, as it is this day, to save much people alive.

Genesis 50:20 (KJV)

---

[1] All Bible Quotes in "We Survive to Thrive" come from the King James Version

We Survive to Thrive

Paula Smith Broadnax

A TRIBUTE TO ERNESTINE "ERNIE" McMILLAN

a dear friend to many...written by her daughter

IT'S NOT ABOUT YOU

By

Kim McMillan-Davis

It was mid-morning on a weekday in March 2001 when my Mom, Ernestine "Ernie" McMillan called and asked if I could take a coffee break so she could stop by. At the time I was self-employed and running my business out of my home. "Yes" I replied. "I'll put a pot on now".

Shortly thereafter she arrived, impeccably dressed as usual and we greeted each other with our normal kiss on each cheek and a hug as we always did. We sat down at the dining room table and I poured us both a cup of coffee.

After we added our cream and sugar, she sat up straight in her chair, clasped her hands on the table in front of her and said "I've been diagnosed with breast cancer". She had just come from the doctor's office, which was nowhere close to where I lived and driven straight to my house to deliver the news.

For some reason neither fear nor anger was my first emotion. Instead a "fight" spirit arose in me and I looked at her and said "You know this is not about you Mom. It's about all of the people whose lives will be touched by your journey." I believe from that moment on she was on a mission.

Although Mom was diagnosed at stage 3 with a very aggressive form of breast cancer, she told me she never once thought about dying. It may seem hard to believe but let me tell you a little about my Mom.

She was born in a little town in West Virginia called Jenkin Jones. (Yes, there really is such a place as I have had the opportunity to visit.) When Mom was five years old, her mother was diagnosed with tuberculosis (TB). In those days there was no cure therefore patients were quarantined. My Mom and her brother were sent to live their mother's sister and her husband in Washington, DC during this time. They had no children of their own but took them in. Later when Mom was 12 years old, her mother passed away from TB. She had been quarantined and separated from her children for all those years.

My Mom and her brother would continue to be raised by their aunt and uncle whom I have only ever known as "Grandma and Granddaddy". They later had a child (daughter) of their own whom my mother loved as her baby sister. Mom grew up and at an early age married and gave birth to my older brother but would later divorce. She raised my brother on her own until she met and married my father. I was the first born of that union and later came my younger brother. But the marriage to my dad was a physically abusive one that lasted over 16 years. The marriage finally ended after an attempt on her life was made by my dad that would play out like something befitting of the Oprah Show. But she SURVIVED!!!

So it was no wonder that when cancer came calling, she went into "survivor mode" and came out fighting for her life. It was what she had done all her life.

Surgery to perform a lumpectomy was scheduled, however during the operation, it was discovered that the cancer was more extensive. After speaking with the surgeon Dr. Rogsbert F. Phillips-Reed from the operating room, it was decided that a mastectomy would be done instead.

I remember the surgeon agonizing over how Mom would feel about waking up without her breast. I assured her that we had discussed this and her wishes were for a mastectomy to be performed should this situation arise. When Mom came back from recovery, I gave her the news that a mastectomy had taken place. She was fine stating the very words she had stated the night before when we prayed for her and the surgeon. "Whatever needed to be done to preserve my life is what I wanted." After the surgery, there were many rounds of chemo-therapy treatments spread out over several months. We were all prayerful but it was during that time my Mom's faith increased. You could tell her every step was by faith. She had made the decision to put this in God's hands and she trusted Him completely.

Dr. Phillips-Reed, who is the founder of "Sisters by Choice", a group that supports women and men diagnosed with breast cancer invited her to a support meeting. She was eager to attend but was a little tearful at the first meeting. What she found there was compassionate support and a loving sisterhood. The meetings were very informative and she took each morsel of information and mixed it with her faith to make it thru her journey.

There were many challenges with the chemo treatments and Mom even had to be hospitalized once. But she was such a fighter. She stood on the promises of God and was relentless in her pursuit of healing and recovery. She would say "breast cancer is being tough with me so I'm gonna be tough with breast cancer." She always wore a smile and constantly encouraged others. I remember her "sending" Dr. Phillips-Reed home to get rest when she made her evening rounds. She was always so thoughtful of others and concerned about their wellbeing. It didn't matter that this was the doctor in charge of her healthcare. She felt an obligation to be concerned and pray for her as well.

With the completion of chemo treatments several rounds of radiation treatments followed. The treatments were as aggressive as the cancer and only by the grace of God, the cancer went into remission! My Mom felt obligated to tell everyone about the goodness of God and the audacity of hope and faith.

She sat out on a journey to walk with others who were starting the journey. She was compassionate and very diligent about staying in touch with others by phone and/or visits. It wasn't unusual for her to be on the phone praying or just giving words of encouragement late at night or early in the morning to someone who was afraid or feeling down. Often times someone needed a ride to or from a doctor's visit. If she couldn't do it herself, she'd make phone calls until she found someone who could.

She became so involved with Sisters by Choice that when the opportunity became available, she became the facilitator. She was adamant about arriving early to set up the room for the meetings. She always had refreshments for the ladies when they arrived. What they didn't know was prior to their arrival she would pray up the room to create an atmosphere of healing and support. Each meeting always ended with prayer.

One thing me and my siblings used to always say about our Mom is "when you come to see 'Ms. Ernie' you can always get (you) some nourishment and some encouragement"! I believe Mom was operating in her calling and ministry. Mom didn't just stop there. She became a member and advocate of the National Breast Cancer Coalition. Every year she faithfully travelled to Capitol Hill to lobby for breast cancer research. There she met with State Congressional leaders and representatives seeking funding for research and quality healthcare. She raised funds for numerous organizations by participating in Walk/Runs for Sisters by Choice, The American Cancer Society and Susan G. Komen.

She went on to form "Ernie's Butterfly Assistance", a foundation to help others thru the journey monetarily. Whether it was to pay a light bill or to buy groceries or gas for your car, she and her foundation were there to assist.

Then one Sunday afternoon I received another call from Mom asking if she, my brother and nephew could stop by on their way home from a birthday party. After they arrived, my husband and I settled on the couch across from her. I watched intently as her demeanor changed and just like before, she sat up straight with hands clasped in front of her and said "It's not good news guys. The cancer is back and this time it's re-staged in my liver."

This time a plethora of emotions ran thru me. You see it had been 10 years since the original diagnosis so I felt "insulted" that we had made it past the "seven-year mark" the doctors always tell you about only to be faced with this again! But then I felt a sense of peace.

You see, the truth is it was a miracle that Mom had survived the first time. The cancer was so aggressive and the stage was so high. That along with the majority of her lymph nodes, which provides direct access to the blood stream invaded by the cancer, could very well have taken her then. BUT GOD!!!

The way I see it, this is my Mom's testimony of just how faithful and awesome our God is. I remember sharing one of my favorite scriptures found in Psalm 91 with her. "He who dwells in the secret place of the most high shall abide under the shadow of the Almighty." I believe my Mom found that "secret place" and found refuge in The Most High God. She knew and understood God's name and trusted Him completely. And He was true to His word. He gave her a longer life, when she called Him, He answered and set her in a place of honor just as He promised in that scripture.

My Mom answered the call of The Most High when she transitioned peacefully from this life on the last day of the 7th month in 2012. Seven is the number of completion. I believe this was God's way of saying "It is finished". Her purpose here on earth was fulfilled and her assignment was completed.

Mom truly dedicated her life to serving others. She was a living demonstration of Christ in the earth. There are those who might say my Mom lost her battle to cancer. I say she definitely won and showed so many others how to win also. My Mom loved butterflies. You couldn't visit her home or office without noticing the presence of them. The butterfly is a symbol of change or transformation and faith. As it transforms from caterpillar to cocoon, the butterfly emerges as a thing of beauty, grace and elegance. This describes my Mom perfectly. She embraced the changes in her life by faith with such grace and elegance. And she was beautiful both inside and out.

So you see this is not a sad story, but instead a story about an incredible woman who did extraordinary things. It's a story about transformation, faith, love and courage. Mom's life symbolizes a call for us to keep our faith as we go through life's transitions. My Mom truly believed she could do all things through Christ who gave her strength each and every day. Even in the wake of her cancer diagnosis, Mom had a huge "to do" list of services to people in need.

Whether it was volunteering at a shelter for battered women, facilitating a support group or helping indigent women obtain free mammograms, she worked tirelessly. The tenacity with which she lived her life gives me strength and encourages me daily.

I pray her story will do the same for you as well.

ABOUT THE AUTHOR

Kim McMillan-Davis is the daughter of Ernestine "Ernie" McMillan. She resides in Snellville, GA with her husband of 26 years and five year old grandson. She is the mother of two daughters.

Kim is an underwriter for a major mortgage corporation. Volunteering and serving others are her passion. Kim is also a seven-year breast cancer survivor and a 17-year survivor of Multiple Sclerosis. She enjoys spending quality time with her family, reading and travelling.

Paula Smith Broadnax

Glenda Atkinson

Georgia

23 Year Survivor/Thriver

ABOUT THE AUTHOR

Glenda Atkinson resides in Lithonia, GA. She took an early retirement from AT&T as an Equal Opportunity and Management Employment Manager before moving to Georgia from Denver, Colorado. Glenda again retired from Encompass Insurance, a subsidiary of Allstate Insurance.

She has been married to Morris for 16 ½ years and together they have five sons, five grandchildren and two great grandchildren. Glenda enjoys reading, being actively involved in the Cancer Support Ministry at her church, and singing in her church choir.

One of her favorite songs is "STAND" sung by Donnie McClurkin. It expresses her thoughts as she deals with thriving past the journey, "YOU JUST STAND AND WATCH THE LORD SEE YOU THROUGH; YES, AFTER YOU HAVE DONE ALL YOU CAN DO – JUST STAND."

2

CHAPTER 1

HAPPY BIRTHDAY

by

Glenda Atkinson

It was a beautiful day in the lovely city of Denver, Colorado. I walked slowly into the Kaiser Permanente Health Office. It was August of 1990 and I wondered "WAS IT MY TURN?" No, No, it was not my turn. I had already had three benign biopsies since 1977. Today is my birthday; I am not receiving bad news on my birthday. HAPPY BIRTHDAY GLENDA, YOU HAVE BREAST CANCER. It WAS my turn.

I am an only child with a Mother who died of cancer in 1978. Our family is uniquely small. My parents were also only children and both their mothers died at an early age. My sons were away from home and my husband was comforting but had other agendas. Unfortunately, I was not as spiritually connected as I should have been. I did not know any women going through breast cancer, so I chose to keep this diagnosis as private as possible. In 1990, breast cancer was not discussed as openly as it is today, so I felt somewhat alone. I was sure I would have no more than five years to live. My heart was heavy and I was worried that my life would not be the same.

My research was limited, but I knew I wanted a mastectomy. My surgery went well and I was told that my lymph nodes were clear and it was caught early. Chemo or radiation was not necessary unless I wanted to do it on a preventive basis. It was truly by the grace of God that He let me live not the five years, but 23 years cancer-free! I feel that God wanted me to grow in faith and help others going through the journey. I am thankful for His blessings.

Too many women get caught up or focus on not being whole; please remember you still have your beauty and femininity. I had those feelings as well. Now I say "Be proud and accept this journey and thank God everyday as you move forward."

In 1992, I moved to Atlanta, GA after divorcing my husband. I joined Greenforest Community Baptist Church and became a member of the Cancer Support Ministry. Through this Ministry, I was able to grow and share as we offered to meet the needs of others on the journey. I accepted the Co-chairman responsibility of the group in May, 2013. We had an event to celebrate for individuals at the church who were cancer survivors. It was to be a very positive celebration focusing on everyone seeing another birthday. I was adamant that this would be a happy time, but I was really heart- broken because a lump had been found just a couple of weeks prior to this event. I put on a "HAPPY FACE" and proceeded with a wonderful celebration, not sharing the news. I had become complacent and thought I might have been home-free.

I realized it was again my turn, and it was God's grace that brought me through those many years, so I began to share.

Sharing my story was complicated and not easy because I consider myself a very private person. I had gone for my yearly mammogram and the nurse informed me that I would have an ultrasound in addition to the mammogram. I thought this was not the usual procedure. I was not having any problems and to my knowledge it had not been ordered. You see I know now it WAS ordered! It was ordered by God. I give God the glory because it was the ultrasound, not the mammogram that saw the small lump on my left breast. I proceeded with scheduling a mastectomy on my left side as it was determined to be malignant.

In 1990, reconstruction was being done. However at that time, I was just afraid to tackle the procedure, so I chose not to have it done. This time (2013), I was advised I could have it done on both sides; making me whole again after 23 years. After the first mastectomy, I did not feel complete and I certainly felt that finding someone who would love me for who I am and not have any issues with my physical appearance would be difficult. Again, I was blessed with a loving man who became my husband in 1998. Although I was blessed, I still wanted to be whole/complete again. I decided on reconstruction.

I consulted with a plastic surgeon for this to be done on both sides. The mastectomy went well and the plastic surgeon proceeded with her surgery immediately after the mastectomy was done. An expander was placed on my left side and as the doctor proceeded to do the same on the right side, she noticed a small lump on the 1990 mastectomy right side. Needless to say, everything stopped and the general surgeon was called back to remove this new lump which they determined to be malignant. Additional doctors were called in to discuss my issue because they were all unsure where this lump had come from and how long it had been there. To God be the glory that the plastic surgeon was on point enough to recognize that something was wrong. We were all amazed, but so very thankful.

Please be aware that a mastectomy does not always guarantee freedom from the return of cancer. I am a witness. Also be sure to take the gene test if you feel that cancer is prevalent in your family. Our bodies are not the same and what may work with one person, may not work for another. I recommend that as you work through your particular journey you consider taking someone with you. It would be helpful to have a family member with you to take notes and ask questions of the doctors. The process can be so overwhelming and you will not be able to remember everything. Keep in mind that men can have breast cancer as well. My husband has also been through a cancer journey.

I was truly blessed because two malignant lumps were found and removed on each side in July of 2013 and to date nothing has spread. I received radiation on my right side and no chemo. I subsequently had to have the breast expander removed from my left side by the plastic surgeon. Because I had radiation, reconstruction will no longer be an option for me. I am currently wearing a very good prosthesis so I am as whole as I can be. I am satisfied that God has again made a way for me and I am eternally grateful.

God has walked with me through this journey and has taught me that sharing is part of His will for me. I shared with my family and later my church family. They were all very supportive, especially my son who came from San Diego, CA to be with me for an entire month. I know that church, family and friends were praying for me. We need to keep praying for a breakthrough for this disease. God is your best doctor!

Be mindful: *"AND ALL THINGS, WHATSOEVER YE SHALL ASK IN PRAYER, BELIEVING, YE SHALL RECEIVE."* (Matthew 21:22)

My journey hit a bump when I acquired a blood clot in my leg. The cause may have been related to my cancer medicine. It has not been determined. It did cause me to have to administer shots to my stomach for almost three months until I could switch to the pill. I was blessed again to have just a superficial blood clot, not one elsewhere that could cause death.

My journey has been trying and it probably is not over. Only God knows. I am thankful as I say I am doing well now and looking forward to my birthday -- a significant one. God has brought me through and I know **He** is in control. I say HAPPY BIRTHDAY to me as I depend on His Word: ***"REJOICING IN HOPE; PATIENT IN TRIBULATION; CONTINUING IN PRAYER"*** (Romans 12:12) ***"I CAN DO ALL THINGS IN CHRIST WHICH STRENGTHEN ME"*** (Philippians 4:13)

Women, as you make your way through that journey, find your guidance in the promises of God; and... HAPPY BIRTHDAY TO ALL!!

We Survive to Thrive

Gwendolyn Black

Age: 61

Georgia

19 Year Survivor/Thriver

ABOUT THE AUTHOR

Gwendolyn Marion Black is a three-time survivor of breast cancer, with her first diagnosis in 1995. She is the mother of one daughter, Aliza Ronit Black, and has resided in Lithonia, GA for 25 years. She was a registered nurse who worked in Burn Units in Georgia and Florida for over twelve years. She also worked with medically fragile infants and children for fifteen years. After her diagnosis and retirement, she dedicated her free time to volunteering and educating the African-American community of the importance of early detection. If you ask her about her journey, she will tell you, "God is not through with me yet. He still has work for me to do, that's why He keeps on blessing me."

CHAPTER 2

I CAN DO ALL THINGS THROUGH CHRIST

By

Gwendolyn Black

June 1978, what a year! My divorce, my Mom's first heart attack, and now, I am headed for surgery! I found a lump in my right breast months ago, but with all that has been going on, I'm just getting something done about it. I saw a doctor who attempted a needle aspiration without success. He referred me to a surgeon. I was working in Harlem, NY at that time and was referred to the Chief of Surgery at that hospital. Because I had insurance, his staff made my appointment at his Park Avenue office. I would later learn that this doctor was very prominent in the Cancer community. I saw him at his office and surgery was planned at Beekman –Downtown Hospital.

My Mom was having a difficult time with my situation because her mother was just diagnosed with inoperative breast cancer. We believed my grandmother knew she had a problem with her breast for years before her cancer was diagnosed. Now at twenty-five, I was faced with the possibility of having this disease. I believed that I caught my lump early, but it was many months later before I was seen by a physician. Yeah, I knew better, after all I am a nurse who treated patients with cancer and knew the importance of early detection. You know, sometimes they say nurses and doctors make the worst patients. So, I want to prove them wrong.

This was the '70s and the process of surgical diagnosis was different. The patient has a biopsy and while waiting in the recovery room, the surgeon gets the results from a frozen section pathology report. If the results are positive for cancer, you are then told and returned to the surgical suite for a mastectomy. As I waited in the recovery room, my Mom was in the waiting room. I would see her again back in my room. I woke to see her standing in the doorway. She was so anxious that she could not bear to come in. I called to her and she approached the bed, pulled back the sheet to find a pressure dressing over an intact breast. MY RESULTS WERE NEGATIVE!!! PRAISE THE LORD!!!

As a twenty-five year old, I was told there were atypical cells noted in my biopsy and that I should be followed closely from then on. Because of my results and my family history, I was now considered high risk for developing cancer in the future. Following the doctors' advice would be a way of life from now on. It was time now to live life to the fullest. I thanked God for granting me this time. I wanted to do things I had only dreamed about up until now. Being born and raised in New York, I always wanted to live in an area where the weather was more temperate. Florida came to mind. I started making calls, purchasing newspapers from Southern Florida and submitting applications for nursing positions.

In December 1979, I headed to Miami, taking a position in the Burn Unit at Jackson Memorial Hospital. I loved my job, loved the unit, but it was difficult to find a permanent place to stay. This was the year of the Cuban Flotilla and the Miami riots, making it almost impossible to find an apartment. I lived in the nurses' dorm for three months, then with a co-worker for a short time, and finally renting a room in a private home. Never being in this type of situation, I never felt comfortable in any of these living situations. After looking for some place for over eight months, I decided to return to Atlanta. God had something in store for me there so it was back to Georgia.

I started working at Grady Memorial Hospital in the Burn Unit in 1980 and would stay there till 1990. I was a travel nurse and worked in the Burn Unit at Humana Augusta for five years.

My mother, Lilly Jane Ingram Black, had hypertensive heart disease. Back in the '80s, heart surgery was a complicated procedure. My mother shared with me her decision not to have open heart surgery to correct blockages in her heart. She knew this would shorten her life, but as a teen she had many surgeries and spent a lot of time in the hospital to correct problems arising from a broken leg as a child in North Carolina. She was preparing herself, but we, (her seven children) were not ready for the loss of our mother. She died of Congestive Heart Failure at the age of 54 in 1985. We loved her dearly, but God loved her more. Within three months, we also lost her mother, Mary Ella Diggs Ingram, due to Advance Stage Breast Cancer and my father's only sibling, Nicey Black, due to natural causes.

After my Mom's passing, I became the legal guardian for my two youngest siblings who were minors. My Mom had sent my baby sister to Atlanta to live with me six months before her passing. My baby brother came down six months after she passed. I suddenly was the single mom of a toddler, Aliza and two teens, Karen and Eric. LORD, IF I'VE EVER NEEDED YOU BEFORE, I SURE DO NEED YOU NOW!!!

As parents, we grew up with our kids. They learned from us and we learned from them. Learning how to parent is a gradual thing. We made mistakes, learned from them, and got better at parenting over the years. Now how do I become the parent of two teens? I have no experience with teenagers. I have lived in the South since my siblings were five and six years old. They knew me as the sister who lived in Atlanta. I would visit New York once a year for a week or two. Now I'm taking over the role of parent. All I can do is pray that God will give me the strength and wisdom I need to get them on their way.

Both my sister and brother were great students. Born a year apart, they were very close. After losing our mother, they wanted to be together. My Mom had done most of the work raising them, so I rarely had any problems with them. Thank God and my mother for that. It was a financial strain caring for three children. Things were better when I was traveling to work in Augusta, but then I was working six days a week, in order to maintain my household. After graduating from high school, my sister attended Paine College in Augusta, GA and my brother returned to New York. After they graduated from high school, it was time to focus on my daughter who was now in elementary school.

Though the years I kept a check on my breast by having periodic mammograms as I was instructed back in 1978. In 1995, I was working with the DeKalb County Health Department. As a contract employee, I had no benefits. Thankfully there was a program called "BreasTest and More" which provided uninsured women with mammograms for free. I qualified for the program and had my test done. My mammogram showed calcifications and I was sent to Dr. Rogsbert Phillips who worked with the county to provide surgical care for those with positive results. I found out a week after my biopsy that I had DCIS, Ductal Carcinoma In Situ of the right breast, an early form of breast cancer. A lumpectomy was performed and radiation therapy began at Grady Memorial Hospital. I actually wanted to have a mastectomy because of my family history and risk, but the doctors talked me out of it. They thought it was too radical, so I leaned on the Lord.   Psalms 28:7

came to mind, "The Lord is my strength and my shield; My heart trusted in Him." (NKJV).

I was so thankful for all the support I received during this time especially from my girlfriend, Deborah Wallace-Kelley. She walked thru the journey with me and I will forever be grateful. I consider her to be my sister from another mother. Thanks also to Amelia Williams, my social worker at Grady Radiation Oncology, who help me apply for services available in the community. I would find out that we attended the same church and she would be an active part of the Cancer Ministry along with me. I was helped by many great organizations in the community. The American Cancer Society helped with transportation; Georgia Cancer State Aid paid for my treatment at Grady Hospital; and a makeover was done after treatment by "Look Good, Feel Better" sponsored by ACS. These programs are still available for those who are in treatment and might need assistance. It is very important not to put off treatment because you feel you can't afford to pay. Speak to the social worker assigned to the hospital or treatment center in your area, they can help guide you in the right direction.

After I completed my treatment, I became a facilitator with the American Cancer Society, MACCA (the Metro Atlanta Coalition on Cancer Awareness) based out of Morehouse College and Bosom Buddies. I wanted to get all the training and information to be an advocate for the African-American community which has the highest morbidity cancer rates among adults in all categories. My church, Greenforest Community Baptist Church in Decatur, GA had a Cancer Support Ministry headed by two survivors, Sis. Johnnie Cannon and Sis. Libby West. Our Executive Pastor, Rev. Herman Cody felt the need to reorganize the ministry when both leaders suffered a relapse of their disease. I joined the ministry with plans to be part of the educational component of the ministry. The ministry was very active in supporting those in the church and community who were on the journey. I was asked to be co-chair with Shirley Kimber-Robinson and we served together until my relapse in 2005.

It had been ten years since my last diagnosis. I was a little shocked, but not completely surprised. Over the years, I had five-six biopsies due to suspicious mammograms. The last time was a year before. My surgeon wanted to operate six months later, but I refused. Now the problem is in the other breast! I made up my mind that I wanted to have a Bilateral Mastectomy this time. I had shared this with my surgeon before, but when I told him my decision, he was not in agreement. I asked him about my risks and chances of relapse with the mastectomy and he answered my questions as best he could. I was thankful for the information, but I was determined to find a doctor who would understand my wishes.

Emory University Winship Cancer Center is where I would have my treatment. A Bilateral Mastectomy with Reconstruction, followed by chemotherapy and radiation. It was a difficult time in my life. My daughter had a son, AJ (Augustus Jase) who was born with many health challenges. The most serious problem required that he have blood transfusions every two weeks. Children's Hospital of Atlanta was across the street from the Winship Center, so we would schedule my chemo and his transfusions on the same day. During this time, I could not help with my grandson and my daughter had her hands full caring for him. The holidays that year were problematic. He was in the hospital most of November, including Thanksgiving and I was in the hospital between Christmas and New Year's.

My grandson passed on January 28, 2006. We were devastated. My daughter was deeply affected by his death, as was I. Like most people, I questioned God. I'm in the middle of chemo, but I'm in my 50's. Why not take me? We all question God at some point in our lives. It is usually later when we are out of our grief that we realize that God always has a purpose, He has a plan. There was no cure for my grandson. The doctors did not even know why his body did not produce enough red blood cells. All they could do was give him blood transfusions whenever his blood counts were low. Imagine a year old infant getting blood transfusions every two weeks, it's very difficult. God gave us one year and 1 week with him, then He took him home were there will be no more transfusions, no more doctors and no more pain. We believe that we will see him again, bye and bye.

I had to stop chemo for a while to deal with my daughter and my grief. Once I sent my daughter away to live with others in my family. I was able to restart chemo, start radiation and complete treatment that summer. I had all the problems that come with treatment, nausea/ vomiting, diarrhea, poor appetite, hair loss, weakness, fatigue, severe pain, numbness of my hands and feet. I lost teeth, toenails and had radiation burns to my chest. But I was blessed because "His goodness and mercy followed me all the days" (Psalms 23:6). Getting back to life after this diagnosis was slow. Developing neuropathy in my hands and feet required the use of a cane to get around, I still carry one in my car because it still affects my feet.

After two diagnoses and the Bilateral Mastectomy in 2005, I thought I was done with cancer. What I learned was that you live with cancer just like any other chronic disease, such as heart disease, diabetes or hypertension. In 2010 after a routine scheduled PET scan, I had a relapse. This time, the cancer was in my mammary nodes. Radiation therapy was my treatment this time. I always kept my appointments with my doctors and had PET scans as ordered. THIS IS WHAT YOU HAVE TO DO WITH THIS DISEASE! There are times of remission and relapse.

Every time that I have been in treatment, there has been a friend or family member on the journey with me. Many have lost their battle, my sister-in-law Patricia O. Black, my pastor Rev. Dr. George O. McCalep, and friends Orrin Batts and Carmella Wheaton Bell. We traveled together on the journey for a time, but God called them all home.

I know that God is not through with me yet. There are more people to educate, support and pray for. My desire is to do His will for my life, which I now know.   I   CAN   DO   ALL   THINGS THROUGH CHRIST WHO STRENGHTENS ME" - PHILLIPIANS 4:13

Paula Smith Broadnax

Age: 67
Georgia
17 Year
Survivor/Thriver

ABOUT THE AUTHOR

Upon retirement from her 30-year career at AT&T, Paula decided to make her dream a reality after being diagnosed with breast cancer. Paula went on to become a successful innkeeper of a bed and breakfast inn (InnParadise) on St. Croix in the U. S. Virgin Islands. After spending five years on St. Croix living her dream she returned to Atlanta and continued with her entrepreneurial spirit. Paula wrote her first book, Dreams, Hopes and Possibilities...a Breast Cancer Survivor's Story of a Dream Come True. Compelling and powerful, the book details her journey from diagnosis to living her dream. Paula also started her business known as Legacy Creations to inspire others to understand the value of leaving a godly legacy for the world and our families strategically and financially. She recently unveiled Paula's Pearls P.I.N.K. 4 C.U.R.E. Jewelry Collection created to celebrate and support Survivors and Thrivers.

CHAPTER 3

Dreams, Hopes and Possibilities

By

Paula Smith Broadnax

Edited excerpt from:
Dreams, Hopes and Possibilities...a breast cancer survivor's story of
a dream come true
Copyright © 2013 Paula Smith Broadnax
ISBN-13:978-1492109198
ISBN-10:1492109193

The pivotal point in my life (which propelled me forward to live my dream) was the diagnosis of breast cancer in May 1997.

I had been prone to developing cysts in my body causing me to have a hysterectomy early in my 30's. I went into the hospital after a cyst had been aspirated. Following that procedure, I developed a pain in that very area. Upon contacting my doctor, she recommended that it be removed. I was admitted to the hospital for the removal of the cyst. When the cyst was sent to pathology…we got the news. This time, it was different.   Dr. Rogsbert Phillips informed us that it was cancerous! I went numb and zoned out. I think I was in shock! Tommie, my husband, was right by my side, holding my hand and listening FOR me because I could no longer hear anything. I was finally able to collect myself. Once I did, I was able to mumble…."What do we do?"

Dr. Phillips recommended doing a lumpectomy (which is breast conserving operation in which the surgeon removes the tumor together with some normal breast tissue surrounding it). Chemo and radiation were the courses of action also recommended.

I have always been quite healthy. My family called me "pleasingly plump" because of my body structure. I do believe that being "healthy" (that is having some meat on my bones) helped me to move through this experience in a way where I did not appear to be sick. I was so blessed! I do not remember losing my appetite and I did not lose any weight. I cut my hair and began wearing a low afro in anticipation of losing my hair. I must tell you that none of my hair came out. I continued to wear the afro for many years because it was low maintenance and I loved the compliments. I chose to delay starting the treatments because in June 1997, one of the Golden Girls (Terri) was getting married. She was marrying Tommie's (my husband's) brother, whom she had met at our wedding. Of course, I wanted to be a part of her special day. Also, before I started treatments, I felt it would be good for me to get away to meditate and pray. Being the eldest daughter of six children, I had always felt responsible for my family and the world at large. At this point, I felt depleted physically, mentally and spiritually. I had always put myself last and I knew that if I was going to be healed....I must begin to think of myself first!

I found a monastery nearby. The Monastery of the Holy Spirit is located in Conyers, Georgia, 35 miles east of Atlanta. It was founded in 1944 by Cistercian-Trappist of the Abbey of Gethsemani located near Louisville, Kentucky. The members of this Order are cloistered, which means they do not leave the monastery precincts except when necessary and they take part in no active ministry outside the Abbey. They dedicate themselves to the worship of God in a hidden life within the monastery. They lead a monastic way of life in solitude and silence, in constant prayer and joyful repentance. Five times each day, beginning at 4:00 a.m., they assemble for community choral prayer. Another one of the Golden Girls (Margaret) insisted on joining me because she did not want me to be alone. I am so glad that she came with me. It was one of the most spiritual encounters I have ever had….the quietness, the early morning prayers, chanting, the lake and ducks. We were even a little mischievous, which lightened the moments. Late one night, we became very hungry so we snuck down to the kitchen to get a peanut butter and jelly sandwich (on delicious, homemade bread made by the Monks). We hurriedly made our sandwiches; scurried back to our room; jumped on the bed and devoured our delicious sandwiches as we giggled!

When we left the Monastery, I was ready to go fight the cancer battle and I knew "We would win!"

Chemo began...it was not easy! Eight weeks of treatment...weekly checkups to monitor my blood count and then the unthinkable happened.....My port got infected after the first treatment! I was devastated because it meant that it must be surgically removed and the wound left opened so that the infection could clear.

Now, I must admit that I am a wimp and queasy when it comes to blood, needles, etc. Walking around with an open hole in my chest was ghastly. Thank God for a strong husband! I believe he was practicing being a doctor on me because he handled every challenge with valor and even seemed to enjoy doing so☺.

I cannot imagine going through this experience without him in my life. It has been my experience that God sends you who and what you need right on time. After about a month of healing, I re-entered the hospital to have the port inserted again. Then the radiation began. The body mold was made to ensure that I remained still during the treatments so that the proper area was treated each time. This was daily for two weeks. That was an experience in itself. My breast actually burned black and the top layer of skin peeled off! Our bodies are amazing and the skin replaced itself with the chocolate brown it had previously been.

The only way I was able to bear this experience is because I was surrounded by so much love. Someone was always available to do whatever was needed. I never went to an appointment or treatment alone. My husband, sons, family and friends were always with and there for me. My youngest son, Kyle, was extremely concerned about my well-being. I cannot thank him enough because he made himself available to go to most of my appointments. He loves me so much and I love him more.

My pastor from my church in Louisville, Kentucky even came to see about me. My co-workers came to visit and see what I might need. My inner circle was and is very tight. I was surrounded by lots of love and support which allowed me to focus on myself and my healing.

After I finished chemo and radiation, I claimed my healing and felt compelled to move forward with the vision that God had given me. I was slightly concerned that it was possible that I would not live to see my dream become a reality.

I was about to turn 50 and near the completion of a 30-year career with AT&T. But there was one thing that needed to be addressed. I felt that I needed my mother's permission to move on. I did not feel like I could leave her. My mother had lived with me for most of my adult life. Tommie and I talked with her and she gave us her blessing. She told me that I had taken care of everyone else all of my life and now it was time for me to do what I wanted. She was so full of wisdom and has instilled a strength in me that keeps me going today.

After much prayer (and I had plenty of time to commune with God during this healing time), I believed that it was time to retire and move forward with the vision of establishing the inn. Several things had become very apparent to me:

1. I was not Mother Teresa and responsible for the world.

2. I should consider putting myself first instead of last.

3. Finally, time was not promised to me.

After much discussion with my husband, we agreed that it was time to move forward.

My dream became a reality in December, 2000 when we were blessed to purchase a lovely, lodge-type home, on a hill, with a million dollar view!! It overlooked the Caribbean Sea and Christiansted town. Once the first guests arrived, it was real to me!! People are willing to pay for what we will give to them even if no pay was involved. For me...it was (and is) all about the HOSPITALITY (which is one of my spiritual gifts).

The scripture that my Mother lived by and passed on to me (and I still live by, even today) is: Hebrews 13:2 (NIV) *"Do not forget to show hospitality to strangers, for by so doing some people have shown hospitality to angels without knowing it."*

Unbeknown to me, the inn was actually our ministry. It created and became a place for people from around the world to: Mark 6:31 (KJV) *"And he said unto them, Come ye yourselves apart into a desert place, and rest a while..."*.

The first guests arrived on April 12, 1999. We were not officially opened for business; but the gentlemen had been ill and his wife felt a trip to the islands was just what he needed. "InnParadise" guests came from around the world. Most came looking for a place to nourish their minds, bodies and/or spirits. It was evident that for the majority, their needs were met and they left feeling much better than when they had arrived.

Fast forward.....it is now 17 years later and I am still here....to God be the glory!! It is my belief that my purpose is "To share with the world that when God created each of us that He placed a dream within our hearts." Something that only WE can do like WE do it! Our mission in this life is to determine what it is or why we are here. Then, move forward (in faith) to make that dream a reality....doing it in a way that God is glorified. In doing so, we will then realize that we are living our purpose or living our destiny.

If you are not living your dream, I encourage you to do so. Have a sense of urgency! Do not wait until something traumatic happens (like a cancer diagnosis) to propel you forward! Go ahead and move from your DREAM TO YOUR DESTINY!

We Survive to Thrive

Yvette Brown

Age: 52

Georgia

9 Year Survivor/Thriver

ABOUT THE AUTHOR

Yvette was born on the beautiful island of Barbados. She currently resides in Atlanta Georgia with her husband of 14 years, Leonard. Employed by American Airlines for 27 years, her life has been enriched by traveling the world and meeting people of all cultures and nationalities.

Her life goal is to share the wisdom, strength and courage which have come to her from being a cancer survivor. To her, a life well lived is to be rewarded with the knowledge that one life has breathed easier because her story has touched it.

Yvette loves to start her day with a Zumba workout and embraces life with laughter, music and dancing.

CHAPTER 4

The Sky Is the Limit

By

Yvette Brown

I never said "Why me? .... It was me. At age forty-three, I was facing my mortality and decided to do it head on. I awoke the day after my diagnosis and thought, "Oh my! Can my husband handle this?" My thoughts were on how this would affect him. So, I called his mother. She said: "Absolutely! My son can handle this. Just get yourself well. He can handle this; and I was never disappointed. God is my salvation but my husband was my rock!"

I know every issue in our lives has a beginning. My issue began right after my mom passed away from multiple myeloma

39

(bone cancer). Her journey was long and painful; but I was there every step of the way --two years to be precise. They say that stress is a silent killer -- it is indeed.

Mom lived in New York and I lived in Atlanta and worked as a flight attendant in Dallas, TX. For two years, my world was consumed with seeing my husband, seeing my mom, and back to work. Atlanta-New York-Texas-Atlanta on my days off! However, I wouldn't have done it any other way.

Mom passed away quietly but that would be the most riveting memory of my life. I fell asleep at her bedside holding her hand and awoke to the tightest grip ever and a cold hand. It didn't sink in until I looked towards the door and in the doorway was a silhouette of Mom waiting to say goodbye. I didn't realize she had died until that moment.... I said goodbye Mom and she was gone. Mom's journey ended and mine begun.

Months later, I lay in bed with my husband with a piercing pain under my right breast. It seemed to be happening repeatedly at bedtime and almost every night. I was constantly telling him it hurts and felt strange until finally he said, "Will you stop telling me (whining) and please go check it out?" What I felt was very tiny and very illusive. The mammogram visit did not show any problems which led me to ask my doctor to touch the area in question. He felt the lump with guidance from me and decided to perform a sonogram. The sonogram did reveal there was a smooth, rounded, solid nodule which was felt to be benign in appearance. He was still not convinced. He told me that it didn't have the consistency of a tumor and that tumors are not supposed to hurt.

This day was one of the most important days of my life and I didn't know it. Why? Because my options were to come back in six months or take it out and have it biopsied. My first and only thought was another six months of complaining about the pain and this feeling will surely drive my husband crazy. So I opted to have a biopsy. I'm so glad that I did!

The procedure was relatively painless and the doctor assured me that from the looks of it, I should be fine; but, really? Six months? Who knows what would have happened while I waited six months.

I drove miles in downtown traffic for my results without my husband because I felt confident that my doctor was right. Big mistake! I didn't have to wait very long (which unnerved me a bit) because the doctor was waiting for me. I've always been the one waiting on the doctor - "Oh boy!" His first statement was "I apologize, Mrs. Brown. In my 27 years as a surgeon, I've never told anyone that it's not Cancer and it is!" I instantly felt a chill run down my spine. I heard my husband asking if I needed him to go with me and me telling him no. Those were the last words I heard clearly. The bit that I heard was "pathology report." What did he just say? Did he say mastectomy or lumpectomy? What did he say? I was numb! I was looking into his face; but wasn't seeing him. I got up overwhelmed with information that made no sense. I made it to my car, navigated traffic in tears and made it home ...but how? Wow ....this was truly the start of my journey.

My support system was full on. My Dad and sisters took shifts flying in to be there for me. November 2, 2005 -- What a memorable day! I was diagnosed with stage one, grade three infiltrating ductal carcinoma in-situ, 0.9cm in size. The tumor was both DCIS and evasive. Because of the evasive nature of the carcinoma 14 lymph nodes were removed and tested, but they were negative -- no evidence of metastasis.

Although I was told my cancer was treatable, the questions remained. What do I do now? Nothing made sense anymore. I'm remembering my Doctor and me discussing my exercising and eating healthy. He believed it was most likely stress related...You think!!

One of my girlfriends was very unhappy with the fact that at the time I was a member of an HMO and my medical team seemed so impersonal. She immediately got me an appointment with the renowned breast surgeon, Dr. Rogsbert Phillips-Reed in Atlanta for a second opinion. How this happened is still a mystery! From the moment Dr. Rogsbert Phillips-Reed entered the room, I looked at my husband and knew instantly that all my questions were going to be answered. She was poised, confident and direct. No more fear! No more panic -- ok I'm ready!

After further consultation with the American Cancer Society and other support groups, the decision was made. My surgery was scheduled. It was decided it would be a lumpectomy. I now needed a break from thinking. What a hard decision that was. Yes, I know I said it time and time again, but it's begun. No looking back. Today is the first day of the rest of my life. Does that make sense?

I've tried to remember to say this quote every day. "God grant me the serenity to accept the things I cannot change, the courage to change the things I can, and the wisdom to know the difference." Wow--what an impact that had on my state of mind. I felt positive amidst my constant fog.

Today is my first MRI. I'm having a bad day because I'm stressing about the machine-- can we say claustrophobic? I've discovered I have a serious case of it even though I've been a flight attendant for 25 plus years and practically live in a tube (plane).

Confined spaces freak me out. I'm so nervous. I was shaking like a leaf, making the test impossible. The technician was kind and gentle, but more importantly -- patient. Finally, after numerous attempts with no success, she invited my husband into the room to hold my hand. I didn't know that was possible, but there he was enduring the loud banging without earplugs, holding my hand. He had no idea what just being there and holding my hand meant to me.

For my pre-op once again, guess who was holding my hand again? His mother was, right! He's got this! The day of my surgery both my hands were held -- Lenny and my sister, Annette. What a blessing! The love and support did not surprise me because that's how my family and I live.

After a couple of weeks of recuperation, I'm now backing to the office of my medical oncologist with more decisions to be made. What is wrong with me? I do not understand anything that is being said. I definitely need a second set of ears! So, I do. It's now my sister, Cheryl, to the rescue.

I feel like I've always had a great deal of faith and with my illness, I know I have to dig even deeper. I am going to pass this test. Being an "over"-analyzer, I spend more time than the average making a decision. But I feel confident that when it's made, it is the right one. Of course, another visit to Dr. Rogsbert Phillips-Reed was needed to validate my decision. My chemotherapy regimen was scheduled for about four weeks after surgery. We had planned for systemic chemotherapy, four cycles of Adriamycin and Cytoxan, followed by four cycles of Taxol. It would be administered 21days apart and followed by eight weeks of radiation. One day at a time, Yvette-- one day at a time!

Even though I have thanked God every day for, a wonderful supportive family, my friends played a huge role in my journey, as well. I met Katrina through a co-worker. At the time, she was a two-time breast cancer survivor. Talking about mentor! I never grasped the full concept of that until now. She lived in Nashville, but I knew I could always depend on her daily call. She was positive and strong and had an overwhelming knowledge of cancer and wellness.

In preparation for chemotherapy, a heart test had to be done. It's called a MUGA Scan along with pre-chemo lab work. Is my heart strong enough? Blood is good? We are on track? People, my heart was good and blood was good (check).

The day before my first chemo cycle, Lenny and I debated on whether we should cut my hair. That was a decision I didn't want to dwell on too long. It's a no brainer! I'm going to lose it anyway. Off to the barber I went. It wasn't the loss of hair that concerned me most. It was the trauma and the drama of how you lost it. As they say, "I didn't want no drama!"

It was decided that I had awesome veins, so no chest port was needed (or at least, not now). Today is the big day -- first chemo cycle, round one. My cocktail (Adriamycin) was referred to as "red Kool-Aid!" It's not so bad .or, at least I though. I felt ok the following two or three days. I was able to run errands, cook, and clean. Maybe, it's not as bad as they say. It was not until the second week after I received it, that occurred to me how potent that stuff was. For me to loss my sense of taste and feel numb and tingly all over this was intense. And oh man --the smell of the chemo! Not good! And, yes -- my urine is red! That stuff is really strong! Oh well, one down seven more to go. Within that 21 days period, I wondered why so long of a wait? But I found out it is different because each individual requires different frequencies and chemo strengths. Every day, I felt a new sensation. It's continuously working. Today, I'm tired but don't feel like I can stay in bed all day. I'm going to run an errand, I thought. So much for that thought. I should have stayed in bed.

Wham! What the heck hit me now? It's evident that it's removing everything in its tracks- the good, the bad, and the ugly. I'm tired and I'm weak.

It's now Christmas Eve day. No, I'm not at all prepared. I woke up with a headache and a stomach ache. The nausea pills they gave me actually seem to work ....Hallelujah! I do feel a little better. It's Christmas Day. I am thankful to have been blessed to wake up and see another bright, beautiful sunny day. Lots of calls today but more surprises are in store for me. I'm overwhelmed again; but this time, with gratitude to my girlfriend, Margie, who cooked my Christmas dinner (no questions asked). That truly made my day! Even though I'm elated with the outpouring of love and kindness, I'm having difficulties getting out of bed and getting dressed and what now! The left side of my face feels stiff, the muscles are unresponsive. Is this a side effect of the chemo or the steroids? Well, nothing is going to stop me from enjoying dinner. I did enjoy it. Man it was good! And Christmas was good. "It's all good."

I was nauseated most of the time, but had to maintain my starting weight throughout the chemo treatment. I had lost weight and then successfully regained it. This is getting hard....God give me the strength.

This is when alternative medicine was introduced to me. I decided to try the holistic approach -- no, not as a treatment for my cancer; but a treatment for my mind, body and soul. I wasn't about to compromise the treatment I had already committed to. My holistic doctor decided on a regiment of vitamins which would not interact, but aid with my nutrition. If I wasn't getting nutrients through food, I had to get it another way ....right? Of course, my oncologist was kept informed of everything I took.

The treatment was progressing somewhat uneventfully and it's now New Year's Eve. We are getting all dressed up and going to a party. I pulled the wig off. I went without a hat--just my little Afro. It's going to be a New Year - a new me!

On New Year's Day, it was a new me alright...oh, oh! What hair I had left was all over the pillow. Instead of having patches, Lenny decided to shave my head bald. I think he had fun playing barber. In the days to follow, all my hair was gone, brows and everything...all of it yawl! That was an experience in itself. How old am I again five?? It sure looks that way. Being five is not so bad ...my skin looked awesome! Maybe there is a silver lining. My vitamins are working, but the chemotherapy is doing exactly what it's supposed to. I have most of the side effects listed; i.e., nausea, vomiting, low blood count, hair loss, and sore mouth. I also had a lot of joint pain. I am not sure if it is related, but both wrists and knees hurt. You name it -- I had it.

Second cycle-- round two! With round one, I was able to eat on somewhat a regular routine even with the nausea...this time not so much. So, I'm here waiting for my cocktail (not feeling strong at all) and I couldn't eat. Today I don't like where they inserted the intravenous. It hurt the entire procedure! I'm miserable and frustrated; but endured it anyway. Of course, days later I was plagued with overwhelming exhaustion. I had no energy! Sometimes not even the strength to talk so I never called anyone. Instead, thank God my friends loved me enough to call and try and keep my spirits up. I'm blessed with the most wonderful friends in the world and I know it.

Another discovery was a rash under my arms, and lingering pain in my chemo arm. Every day, there were new symptoms. I can cope with them though and I had better, I still have a ways to go.

I had an appointment with my holistic doctor today. Through several tests that he performed for my treatment process with him, he discovered that my problem stemmed from emotional traumas more so than physical. A few came to mind, so I had to agree with him there. I'm proud of myself that I persevered. However, not without some scars and my illness to prove it. At first, it appeared that I was only weak and tired a few days after the chemo cycle. However, now it seems it's taking the entire 21 days for my body to prepare for the next round. I have headaches which seem to only to occur when I lay down. So we've decided I was going to sleep standing up. Ha-ha!

My third cycle! Whew... it's round three and there are good days and bad days, mostly bad days. The reason I call them rounds is because it feels like I'm in a ring with a boxer and he thinks he is going to win. But I know no matter how badly I'm beat up, I will be the champion. It can sometimes make you nervous and worried because in the effort to heal your body, chemo poisons it as well, damaging vital organs. Did I mention that one of the major side effects is congestive heart failure? Wow!! The stress on your body is incredibly harsh. I'm now seeing my holistic doctor on a regular weekly schedule. It is more important now, more than ever, that I eat the right foods and take supplements. I'm still suffering the effects; but without supplements, I would have no strength at all some days. Plus (yes there are some pluses) my holistic doctor is a chiropractor and the highlight of my visits were the spinal adjustments. I always felt like I was walking on air when I left the office. I felt like it kept me centered and at oneness with my body, even with the chemo beating I was getting.

I had promised that being concerned about stuff to cover my bald head was the least of my problems, but its winter and my head is freezing! It is wig shopping day. The wig shop I went to is specifically geared towards breast cancer survivors and other hair loss illness. This is incredible. I have never seen this many wigs in my life. Fun, fun, fun! I picked a few ranging in different lengths and colors. I'm so excited about having a fun new look.

Prior to each cycle of therapy, lab work had to be done. My scheduled test showed that my white blood cells were critically low, but not enough to hospitalize me. Thank you, Jesus! Instead, I was sent home with medication to inject for three days on every other day. I'm injecting myself! Scary! Neupogen helps the body make white blood cells and prevents infection during the treatment. Do I want to do it—no!   Do I need to do it—absolutely! I'm uncomfortable about injecting myself; but like everything else I've had to do thus far -- I can do it.

And, now for the dreaded word paperwork! I think I've put it off long enough. Insurance, medical and personal have to be in place. It's important for your healing process to not have to worry about how the bills will get paid. I won't capitalize on the insurances, but if I didn't have some at the time, what a much harder recovery that would have been.

Today, I looked at myself in the mirror. I have dark circles under my eyes. My fingernails and toenails are darkened by the chemo. It's now three days before my fourth chemo cycle. I am exhausted and I have a fever of 106 degrees –That's not good!! I have to see my doctor. It may be just another side effect, but I would hate to delay my treatment. I was given medication and we are back on schedule.

Hey, by the way, I'm still receiving my cocktail intravenously in my left arm. It hurts, it's sore, and it gets really stiff at times; but my vein is holding up....Yeah! I hope. Today we are going for another arm infusion. I'm starting to get worried about the vein collapsing because of how hard it has become. It was no longer plump and visible. It was now hardened. How much more can it take. I tell myself everyday how beautiful and strong I am and I could do this. I am doing it.

My diet was very strict. I think I need to make some changes in order to see what works and what doesn't. I am now eating foods like, steel grain oats; lots of fruits and vegetables and I have started juicing. Even though I am still nauseated, I was vomiting less frequently. I'm still in a bad place with how rotten chemotherapy makes you feel; but I'm happy for any reprieve.

Since it's been already two months of chemo, I think I have experienced all the different side effects and lost everything that was predicted I would lose. A lot has happened in a short space of time; but, it's best to be prepared for all that can happen and then be pleasantly surprised if it doesn't.

Today is a wonderful day! I'm at the office of my oncologist for my follow-up. He has got really good news for me. I no longer have to continue with the four cycles of Taxol. I was given my progress report to review so I could decide if I wanted to proceed or not. I decided not to proceed and felt good about my decision. I thanked him, my arm thanked him. I was never so happy in my life. I never needed the chest port after all.

Now the next phase of my treatment will commence. The following week my visit with the Radiation oncologist begins. The whole procedure is concentrated on isolating the area where the cancer was removed. So a cast is molded to fit your body. It would protect the surrounding areas and only hit the area intended. It was unreal and kind of scary to see how many casts were in the room (which meant there were lots of other people going through some form of radiation). But I was very optimistic. I've conquered one feat. I'm sure I can conquer this as well.

I know this is not the same kind of poison like chemotherapy. But when you hear the word "radiation" you automatically know that more cells are going to be zapped (destroyed). You go in knowing what to expect; but it always seem to manifest into the unexpected.

I hadn't fully recovered from chemo at this time. I've had about three weeks rest; but it was time to move on. As usual, before any treatment there are a scheduled array of tests, blood pressure and temperature checks, and the whole nine yards. Everything has to work. One thing being off throws you off schedule. I've been given the go ahead. All checks are good. So my Radiation therapy is scheduled for every day, Monday through Friday, with Saturday and Sunday off for eight weeks. It's only a fifteen minute procedure, but I have to drive downtown to have it done in rush hour traffic. No problem -- I'm on a mission. I always give myself plenty of time so I was never rushed, stressed or late. Lenny of course took time off from work to accompany me on some of the visits. During the first week I thought, "What are they talking about?" You are in and out so quickly that you falsely think that surely not much damage can be done.

On the second week, they gave me a topical lotion to apply to the area to aide with the sensitivity, soreness and irritation. Red Alert ... Really, I'm fine. Well, it was sore but I thought that was because of my surgery. That was partially true. Radiation was killing the inner and the outer cells of that area; so it was getting dryer and dryer every day. There was already pain. So it just got more and more painful. Every week I went, I thought to myself, I'm doing very well. The pain is normal, but the other problem that was irritating was the itching in the area with the tapped marking for radiation. It was driving me insane! It's an itch you can't scratch.

They suggested having a buddy accompany you to your treatments. It shouldn't be hard to go to these appointments alone —right?? This is not a 14 hour flight to Japan! It's a 20-minute drive downtown and a 15-minute session. No problem! Oh, but I see why, Man, oh, man -- it was exhausting! It drained all my energy. I wasn't expecting this; but most days after I left my session and went home, I had to sleep. I was totally wiped out.

Around the fifth week, I started to visibly see the changes in my skin in the treated area. The technician always commented on the fact that it was surprising how well my skin looked. But it was taking its toll now. It had started to darken and I could hardly touch it. I was now starting to really understand the affects. I had been applying the lotion religiously; but normal or not, the pain was intense and my skin was burnt by the seventh week. I mean burnt!

The burning and discoloration just started much later than the average. It's not the end of the world. I can overcome this as well. By the end of the eighth week, it was unbearable; but I was determined to win. I knew that this test was bestowed upon me for a reason. I now know who I really am. I know my strengths and my weaknesses. Throughout life we are given numerous tests. Some we are unaware of; but with this kind of test, you summon the courage and you fight. Some are long and some are short, but we fight anyway.

I am taking additional time away from work to rebuild my immune system. I was concerned about getting on an airplane and traveling internationally. My system was far too compromised. So, I continued my weekly holistic visits, started yoga classes; stayed on my new diet of no red meat and lots of fruits and vegetables. Now I can monitor and manage my weight. I've also learned of other tools to detox my body. My road to recovery has started.

What an awesome day, I awoke realizing that it's done, my treatment is really over. I'm constantly smiling at myself in the mirror. I'm so proud of you, Yvette...so very proud. Now my next mission is getting my body back in shape.

I started my workouts -- 10 minutes a day. Ten minutes and I was winded. I couldn't believe it! Trying desperately not to get discouraged, I also started walking with April (my dog) in my subdivision. I made it once around and that to me was an achievement. In two weeks, I was able to increase my workout to 15 minutes and extended my walk. You go girl!

As time went by, I stayed 15 minutes, twice a day morning and evening. This was really working for me. I started to build my stamina. Every day, I felt an improvement until one day I told April "we are walking even further today." It was a long stretch which elevated as we walked. I could see the top of the hill and made that my goal. I made it to the top, but felt ill. My vision was blurred! I was blacking out! I fainted in the street!

It was midmorning, so most of the residents were at work. I never fully lost consciousness; but was too weak to move. When I eventually tried, I felt weighted down. April was sitting on me, protectively and whining. She didn't know what to do. Luckily for me, I always carry my cell phone and it was Lenny's day off. So I called him and he came immediately. Usually when April sees Lenny, she would run to him. But not this day! She was not leaving my side. I had obviously overdone it. I was fine, but I had pushed myself too hard and too fast.

That was just a minor setback; but after a day of rest, I was back in the saddle. I was seeing remarkable changes. I was growing stronger every day and looking great. However, I still felt like there was something missing, something unfinished.

Then it came to me! This has been a journey for Lenny too! No, not near as bad -- but he stood by me, and appreciated it. We need to celebrate! I appreciated it so much that I decided we needed to renew our vows, to say "I do" all over again. When we got married the first time, we eloped. This time I wanted all my family and friends to celebrate with us. So, let the celebration begin.

This would turn out to be my happiest day ever. It was a backyard wedding on August 19, 2006 a week shy of our original wedding day. At that time we had been married six years. Mom was not there; but Dad gladly walked me down the path to Lenny. When Lenny and I reached the arch where the minister stood, I looked up and attached to the arch was the most beautiful picture of my mom. I couldn't help myself -- I burst into tears. She was there with me after all. Whoever thought to do that honestly knew that I was missing my mom that day. What an awesome gift to give me.

I felt like my life went a full circle because of this experience. I also fully understand what "the sky is the limit means." I've been given a second chance with unlimited possibilities. Yes, my career has given me the ability to fly; but I now have the strength to soar.

I am a nine-year survivor! Now I never take anything or anyone for granted because I acknowledge the gift of life I've been given.

Sarah Grant

Age: 61
Georgia
10 Year Survivor/Thriver

ABOUT THE AUTHOR

Sarah Grant is the proud mother of one son, Johnny Lewis and grandmother one grandson, Johnny Kortez Lewis. Sarah, an original Georgia peach, has resided in Georgia all of her life. She is a public speaker and has been the keynote speaker at numerous cancer programs throughout the city. Sarah is passionate about volunteerism and has volunteered with the American Cancer Society for seven years where she served as Chairperson for the South DeKalb Relay for Life for several years.

She also volunteered at the Atlanta Hope Lodge which provides housing to cancer patients during their treatments. She provided counseling to both survivors and caregivers. She was a caregiver to her mother who died of colon cancer. Sarah continues to encourage and support other cancer survivors and caregivers throughout the nation. She is very passionate about cancer awareness and does not take being a ten year breast cancer survivor lightly. Sarah enjoys traveling and currently works for a Fortune 500 financial institution as an Administrative Assistant.

Chapter 5

Cancer Is Not the End – It's A New Beginning

By

Sarah Grant

The word cancer is a scary word. When most of us hear the word cancer, we immediately think someone's life is about to end. I personally found out "Cancer Is Not the End – It's A New Beginning."

My first experience with someone having cancer was with my father about 35 years ago when he was diagnosed with throat cancer. He never complained. I admired how he was always trying to encourage my mother ...trying to prepare her for his leaving her.

During the time of his illness, the full-service service stations were becoming extinct. My father told my mother that he will not leave her until he felt comfortable with her checking the oil in her car and putting gas in it.

My father was in and out of the hospital several times. One night while in the hospital, my father told my mother that he went to Heaven and he described how beautiful it was. He didn't want to come back to Earth but he had to because it was not his time. I believe without a doubt that when you have a relationship with God that He will allow you to see past this earthly realm and He will let you know when time on Earth is about to end.

Each time my father was in the hospital, I was working and when I left my job, I would go directly to the hospital and stay until 9 or 10 p.m. On the day that my father passed away, he had been in the hospital that morning. He told the doctor he did not want to die in the hospital and wanted to go home. The doctor granted him his wish and released him from the hospital. When I got to my parents' home, I immediately start calling medical supply places because the doctor said he would be more comfortable in a hospital bed. Every place I called informed me that they didn't have any hospital beds. My reaction was, – "How could Metro Atlanta not have any hospital beds?" I just couldn't believe it! After making several more phone calls my father told me I should go home and cook dinner for my family since I wasn't cooking much during those days. I told him I didn't want to go and he kept insisting that I leave; so finally I did.

I was home just starting dinner and my phone rang. It was my mother calling to tell me that my father had just passed away. I didn't understand why my father was insisting that I leave, but I believe in my heart that he knew the end of his life was near and he didn't want me to see him take his last breath. I was so hurt that he had died, even though the doctor had told us that they had done everything they could for him. I was hoping we would have had a little more time together; but that was not in God's plan. I was so thankful that my mother was a strong Christian because she handled my father's passing in a very calm manner.

My second experience with cancer was with my mother. She was diagnosed with colon cancer in January 1999. It was a Wednesday evening, I was on my way to Bible Study. It was about 6:00 p.m. and Bible Study didn't start until 7:00 p.m. I decided I would stop by my mother's house and visit with her for a while. My nephew, who lived with my mother, told me that my mother hadn't eaten all day. I asked her why hadn't she eaten and her response was "I'm not hungry and my side hurts a little." Knowing how my mother liked to eat, I knew something was wrong. I told her I was going to go buy her a hamburger and some french fries. She told me not to go because I would be late for my Bible Study. I replied, "Bible Study can wait, I'm going to get you something to eat."

When I returned to my mother's house with the food, she took one bite of the burger and ate just a couple of the french fries and said she was finished. I told her if she didn't eat more, I was taking her to the hospital. She didn't eat any more and I took her to the Emergency Room. The people in the Emergency Room told me I couldn't stay with her in the room and I told them I wasn't going anywhere and I didn't leave.

We arrived at the hospital a little past 7:00 p.m. There were no chairs nearby, so I stood on my feet until around 2:00 a.m. and finally someone brought me a chair. During the time in the Emergency Room, my mother was taken out of the room to get lab work done. They told me they were going to keep her overnight for more testing in the morning. The clock just kept ticking away. Now, the time is around 5:00 a.m. and we are still in the Emergency Room. I asked what was taking so long for them to get my mother into a room. Their response was "We're waiting for a room to get cleaned-up." I replied, "If I need to clean the room, I will." They said it shouldn't be much longer.

Finally, it's about 6:00 a.m. and a room was ready for my mother. I was so tired from having to stand for so many hours and just staying alert for such a long time. Someone came to get my mother for more testing and afterward, they brought her back to the room. An hour or more later, the doctor came in. He informed me that the tests revealed my mother had colon cancer and it was nothing to be alarmed about since he was going to cut out the portion of her colon with the cancer and reattach the colon.

Well, that's what the doctor thought. When they cut my mother open, they discovered cancer was throughout her entire body! The doctor came out of the operating room to talk with me. He started off by apologizing, saying he thought it was just a little cancer and found out differently. He asked if my mother had been complaining of pain in her side and I told him just yesterday she said her side was hurting a little. He was amazed because the condition my mother was in, she should have been complaining a lot. My mother had a high tolerance for pain and so do I.

I was informed by the doctor that my mother would probably live just one month and maybe just a little over. I told the doctor my mother was not going anywhere within a month because she had never been sick in my life and I knew God would not take her from me within a month. My faith in God is so strong that I don't allow man to tell me when life is about to end. They put a colostomy bag on my mother and she was in the hospital for several days. When they released her from the hospital, I informed them that I was going to be her caregiver. Since they didn't show me how to put a colostomy bag on her, I figured it must not be hard and didn't think to ask them if they should show me.

Later that evening, my mother's colostomy bag needed changing and I thought I did it correctly until it started sliding off. Even though I was panicking, I didn't let my mother see it. I called someone who was a nurse and asked her to talk me through how to correctly put a colostomy bag on. The next one I put on didn't come off.

That night when I was praying, I asked God not to let any more of the colostomy bags I put on come off. He granted my wish and no other colostomy bags came off which I put on my mother. God will answer prayers, if you just believe.

During one of the conversations I had with my mother, she said she believed her body was in bad shape and she never wanted to talk about it. My mother was never told in the hospital that she had cancer and after being released from the hospital, we never talked about it. Even though we didn't talk about, I'm pretty sure she knew she had cancer.

Several months passed by and my mother's doctor couldn't believe she was still alive. He requested Hospice personnel to start coming to my mother's house once a day. My mother's appetite was pretty good for a while which means the colostomy bag got full several times a day. Since Hospice was only coming once a day, all of the other times the colostomy bag needed changing, I had to do it. Having to go to work during the time I had to care for my mother was a bit challenging. However, I did what I had to do. I am a praying person and found myself praying two to three times daily just thanking God in advance for the strength He would give me to go through this journey with my mother. I didn't want my mother to die during one of the times I was tending to her body and part of my prayer was thanking God in advance that she would pass away during her sleep.

More than a year passed and my mother was still alive. She definitely beat the odds against her. Hospice informed me that they were going to put my mother on morphine and I told them that she was not going to need it. They informed me that all of their patients take morphine during their last days. I told them, my mother was not going to be in pain because every day that I prayed, I thank God in advance that she would not be in pain and once again God granted my wish. She was never on any pain medicine, not even a Bayer aspirin or Tylenol.

Hospice nurses told me that since I was in denial that my mother was not going to need morphine, I needed to talk with the Hospice doctor. I told them I will talk with anyone they want me to. I will tell them she will not need morphine. Since my mother became a Christian as a child, I had never seen her ill. I just knew God was not going to forsake her now and allow her to be in pain and have me watch her in pain. She was never in pain. My mother passed away on March 30, 2000 peaceably in her sleep.

After her death, I found out the importance of a person having a colonoscopy. If there is a polyp in the colon tract during a colonoscopy, most doctors will remove it immediately to avoid a person getting colon cancer. A polyp has to be in the colon for a while before turning to cancer. Cancer screening is very important. It can make the difference between living longer or dying early.

After my father passed away from cancer and while being a caregiver to my mother, I started thinking, if I was ever told I had the big "C" (cancer), I knew exactly how I would react. I was wrong!

Now, let me tell you about my own cancer. School was out for the summer of 2004. I decided to take my grandson to Florida. My best friend and her granddaughter went with us. I did all of the driving and for the four days in Florida. I had driven about 1,200 miles. During the return trip to Atlanta, I felt pain in my breast. I thought it was due to being in a car for so many miles with the seatbelt across my chest. I wasn't too worried about it since I was already scheduled for my mammogram in two weeks.

I had the mammogram on a Monday and two days later received a call while at work from my primary physician's office informing me my mammogram was abnormal and I needed to see a surgeon immediately to see if I had cancer. They had already made an appointment for me with a surgeon the following day on Thursday. When I hung up the phone, I started thinking, "I may have cancer." I tried holding back the tears. Slowly the tears started coming down. I couldn't believe my doctor's office called me at work to give me the news of the possibility that I may have cancer! I thought that was very insensitive. I picked up my x-rays from the hospital on Wednesday evening because I knew the surgeon would want to take a look at them. I was very nervous while driving to the surgeon's office not knowing what he was going to say.

Upon entering his office, there were no other patients in the waiting area. I immediately thought to myself-- if this is a good Surgeon, he should have a room full of patients. I was escorted to a room where I had to wait for the doctor to come in. After waiting about thirty minutes, he finally came into the room.

My chart was open on the counter and I saw my mammogram results on top. After the doctor entered the room, he asked why I was there. I told him I had an abnormal mammogram a few days ago and brought my x-rays for him to see. He looked strange. I asked him didn't he want to see them and his response was "Since you brought them, I'll look at them." He made me more nervous than I was when I entered into his office. He said, "I guess I should examine your breasts." I responded, "That would be a start." While examining my breasts, he kept looking at the ceiling. I immediately came to the decision that I can't have this man operate on me because I didn't trust him.

He started asking questions. "What should I do?" I told him "He was supposed to be an expert and he should tell me what should be done to confirm whether or not I had cancer." Then he asked which hospital I wanted to go to and I told him. He responded that he liked another hospital. I told him if he didn't want to operate in the hospital I suggested, why ask me where I wanted to go. Yes, you guessed it, I became even more nervous because I was saying to myself, "There's no way this man will perform surgery on me because he will probably kill me."

It is very important that you have complete trust in your doctor and especially when they're talking about performing any type of surgery. I had a conversation with an operating room nurse prior to my mammogram. She informed me that people had died on the operating table from fear that they wouldn't make it. Since I had fear with this doctor, I wasn't about to allow him to operate on me. While driving away from the doctor's office, I thought to myself, I should have brought a friend with me to calm me down. Luckily for me, I was scheduled to see my primary physician the following day. I couldn't wait to see him so I can let him know I did not like that doctor he sent me to.

My primary physician informed me that the clinic was forcing them to refer surgical patients to the other side of town. However, if I wanted to get a second opinion, he would refer me to a doctor he would use if he had to have surgery. I told him if the doctor is good enough for him, he's definitely good enough for me.

My primary physician asked the referral clerk to call this other surgeon to see when I could be seen. She informed my primary physician that I could be seen in two weeks. I advised my doctor I couldn't wait that long. He got on the phone with the surgeon to ask if he could fit me in sooner and he said he would squeeze me in the following Monday morning.

Oh, what a relief that was; knowing I could see another surgeon so quickly. Upon arrival at the second surgeon's office, there were several patients in the waiting area which made me feel at ease. This time, I brought a friend with me. Shortly after being escorted to an examining room, the surgeon came in. He immediately asked if I had brought x-rays and he wanted to see them. He took a pen and paper and drew a breast and told me where he was going to cut me. He said his first step was to do a biopsy to confirm whether or not I had cancer and if I did, what stage it was in. He agreed to perform the surgery at the hospital of my choice. The result of the biopsy revealed I had cancer in the early stage. Also, he said I had a little more than one cm of good tissue around the area and didn't think he needed to perform a lumpectomy. I asked him to do a lumpectomy because I needed to know definitely that I had more than one cm of good tissue, just to have peace of mind.

The result of the lumpectomy was that all of the remaining tissue was good. Since my stage was zero, I only had to take 39 radiation treatments and no chemo. I was relieved that I didn't need chemo. My surgeon and radiologist both told me about the many side effects from radiation and informed me that I would not be able to work while taking treatment. I told them I was sure I would be able to work because God had His Angels watching over me and I would not allow man to dictate what will happen to me.

At the end of my treatment, I was asked by my radiologist how much time could I miss from work. I reminded him that I told him God was protecting me and I wouldn't miss any time from work. He just couldn't believe it. I told him to stop thinking every patient will have the same reaction when in reality, no two people are the same.

I know it was my faith that saw me through my journey and now I know "Cancer is not the end – it's a new beginning." The things I worried about in the past, I don't worry about anymore. Life is good and I'm very thankful to God for my new beginning.

My being a caregiver of someone with cancer and having my own cancer allows me to encourage many people in and outside of Georgia regarding their journey with cancer. Caregivers need to be encouraged just as much, if not more, than the cancer survivor. I'm a firm believer that if you have not walked in my shoes ahead of me, you can't help me through the journey. Experience is the best teacher in everything. Life is meant to be enjoyed and people should focus more on the positive things than negative ones. Your mind is very powerful and after becoming a cancer survivor it made me appreciate life even more than I had been.

There are more than 150 different types of cancer. Some of which people died shortly after being diagnosed. People are living longer, productive lives as a result of extensive cancer research. I tell people "Don't be afraid of getting cancer; be afraid of getting it late." The only way you get it late is you ignore signs your body gives you and you don't go to the doctor for routine check-ups which includes cancer screening. Also, it is important to know your family history since some cancers are hereditary. I have a motto -- "Attitude is Everything."

Each day I wake up is another blessing from God. I will not and cannot take life for granted. I thank God each and every day for allowing me to remain on earth for as long as He has because life is shorter than we think.

Connie Haynes

Georgia
18 Year
Survivor/Thriver

ABOUT THE AUTHOR

Connie Haynes is a native of Georgia and lives in Stone Mountain with her husband of 43 years, Melvin. Connie and Melvin have two adult daughters, Kiera and Deirdre Haynes. Her profession over the past 30 years has involved numerous aspects of Human Resources. Connie retired in 2012. After a year, she returned to work with a staffing agency.

Connie's love and obedience to Christ keeps them active and involved in their local church. Connie loves chocolate, poetry, puzzles, Scrabble and black and white movies.

Chapter 6

"I DON'T BELIEVE HE BROUGHT ME THIS FAR TO LEAVE ME"

By

Connie Haynes

The year was 1991. This was the year when my family moved to Georgia from Virginia after eight years of living in the suburbs of Washington, DC where I had a wonderful church, home, community and friends. My husband, Melvin, and I had two daughters, Kiera and Deirdre. They were teenagers in the last few years of high school and they did not want to make the move. Can you blame them? We are talking about leaving lifelong friends, and missing out on graduation and proms with them. It was a hard time for everybody.

The housing market was slow. The house in Virginia had not sold before we continued on with plans for the move. This meant commuting back to Virginia to check on the house and do required maintenance. Since I was not working, I would occasionally go back to check on the house and attend to maintenance that was needed. The house still held all of our furniture.

The temporary housing we chose was an apartment. This was new for Kiera and Deirdre. They had always lived in a house with a yard and no neighbors attached on each side and on the bottom level.

Teenagers like music, loud TV and other things off sync like running the dishwasher and clothes dryer during evening hours (this doesn't work in an apartment setting). All the stress elements were in place: moving, new job, new school, house hunting, house to sell, and no exercise schedule. I thought the stress elements were under control because I was young, in good physical shape, and pretty much took care of myself – up to that point. I thought that my body could handle that temporary calamity. A temporary life calamity for one person can trigger different physical responses for another (as I would soon find out). My thoughts were that everyone else came first for now. I felt I would get my routine back and everything would fall back in place. Oh, how faulty was my thinking!

Our teenagers finally settled in with new friends at church and school. After a year, the house sold, Melvin found another job, I began to work, and we felt free to buy a home and rental property. I realized I only replaced the former stressful activities with new ones.

It finally dawned on me that I needed to slow down and really commit to checking on myself. I had no negative physical indicators, but I knew I had missed a lot of checkups. Five years had now passed since the Virginia relocation. I don't know how closely I was paying attention to my own body (probably not much at all).

I was no different from other women who had discovered that they had breast cancer. I had previously discovered a nipple that was abnormal (opened outward with a milky residue). My thought was it was baby powder that had become moist around my nipple. But my husband and I felt a lump that had not gone away after a month. That is not natural!

For so long I guess I had started playing the role of "Super Mom or Super Woman" and the annual mammogram appointments suddenly became "now when was my last appointment? As I grew older, I was more attentive an I scheduled my appointments more regularly. During this time, I actually had gotten my exams in the prescribed time period. The healthcare system at that time seemed to encourage basic healthcare, but this was no basic situation. My exams and screenings showed that the breast tissue was dense and hard to indicate abnormalities.

God is so good...and on time all the time! While having a mammogram, I was so blessed to have an x-ray technician who was patient, efficient, and concerned about me. She saw something on the film and conducted an additional angle shot. Her trained eyes just would not let her give up. She called someone and somehow got a doctor to commit to reviewing the film. They both realized there was an irregular and abnormal spot on my breast. With that confirmation, it was now up to the physician to talk to me.

The physician did talk to me over the phone. Without an exam, he decided it was nothing to be concerned about and that I should come back in six months for reevaluation. It was very clear that I was talking to and was getting advice from a "non –caring" and "non-involved" person. He did not deserve to be called a physician! How could he make such a detached statement when the mammogram had confirmed an abnormality? He decided no more attention was required for my situation until another six months. Insurance companies sometime encourage physicians to do a minimum if they plan to be paid. The patient gets to pay the premiums, but gets minimal care under certain healthcare plans.

"The Lord does not give us a spirit of timidity (fear), but gives us a spirit of power, love and a sound mind" (2Tim 1:7).

It was time to move on from a "you can only be seen at certain locations and can be referred to doctors if the primary care physician chooses" type of health care. The Holy Spirit had already led me to sign up for cancer coverage and health coverage under my employer, as well as additional health coverage under my husband's plan during the health benefits open enrollment period. I certainly had chosen a considerable amount of additional coverage that I would normally have tried to minimize...thinking we don't need this...trying to save money.

Now was certainly the time to again listen to the Holy Spirit's guidance for a new physician. I really had no one in mind nor did I have family or friends to refer me. I looked for doctors under my coverage and who were accepting new patients. This process took almost six months (the same amount of time the previous physician wanted me to come back to see him). I felt I was going forward while the previous physician was holding me back.

The new physician carefully examined me and immediately had me set up with a surgeon to do a biopsy. We knew the biopsy results would take a week. We were going to continue with our vacation plans and pray for God's coverage over our vacation and the biopsy results.

Melvin and I had planned our 25th anniversary for months. His job kept him on the road five days a week —spending an abbreviated weekend at home before getting an early Monday morning flight again to start another week. We were so looking forward to our vacation. We took that wonderful seven-day trip to Hawaii and it was just what we hoped it would be. Melvin and I never talked about the impending health concerns during our vacation. We focused on twenty- five years of marriage, two wonderful children, and having fun in wonderful Hawaii.

On our return home, we found that the surgeon had left a voice mail message stating that **we** needed to schedule an appointment to go over the biopsy results. The fact that he requested both of us to come to the office let us know there was a concern. We made the appointment and went to the office. The Holy Spirit was still at work. The night before the doctor visit, I was watching a movie and the major character was a doctor who had been diagnosed with cancer. During the movie, questions were asked and explanations given about cancer stages, surgery and recovery. These were things that I had not thought of or would not have known to discuss with my doctor.

When we went into the lobby of the doctor's office, I cannot remember anyone else being in the lobby but us. This seemed very unusual to me because most doctor offices are full of waiting patients. What I do remember is that we spotted a Bible amongst the magazines on the bookshelf. We found a comforting Scripture and felt at peace with anything the doctor chose to tell us. Our Heavenly Father was in control. We knew that there was nothing that He could not do.

The surgeon said "Yes, the biopsy showed that the lump was cancerous and would need to be surgically removed. My thoughts about having surgery or even having cancer never seemed totally something to fear, because for so long I had been functioning in whatever situation I found myself in. Here again I was following the same—"no time to cry or worry" mindset. I knew that there were situations and other people more important than the concerns that I had. I felt I had to move on –do the necessary—make it right for everyone else—get it fixed—get healthy and get on with it. I knew there was much more coming to me, so to think at age 42 everything would be over for me was not the thinking of a "survivor or thriver".

The surgery was successful. The surgeon performed a lumpectomy on my right breast and removed some of the lymph nodes under my right arm. The treatment after the surgery included five weeks of radiation and medication. I was able to return to work and schedule my five-week radiation treatments after work. Melvin contracted pneumonia and was hospitalized during this time. My treatments and his care were going on at the same time. Still I pushed on to maintain my duties at home and at work. My skin was burned and irritated by the radiation and my strength was drained by its effect as well as my duties at work. God's footprints were truly in our "sand of challenge."

The success, the blessing and hope were already in place. The battle was already won. Since 1996 after completion of two five-year cancer drug treatments and continued follow-up with my oncologist, it is my belief that..."He did not bring me this far to leave me!!!!!"

Gwendolyn Murphy

Age: 62
North Carolina
10 Year Survivor/Thriver

ABOUT THE AUTHOR

Gwendolyn Fox Murphy lives in Wilmington N.C. with her husband of 32 years, Robert. She is the proud mother of one daughter, Alecia. She is semi-retired and volunteers at New Hanover Regional Medical Center in the Cancer Registry. Some of Gwen's proudest accomplishments are being a VISTA volunteer in the 70's and contributing to this book! Gwendolyn loves music of all kinds and loves to read. She is addicted to "Words with Friends" (the board game).

Chapter 7

I WOULDN'T TAKE NOTHING FOR MY JOURNEY NOW

By

Gwendolyn Murphy

The most unique journey of my life began in September 2002. I was a 50 year old child of God, wife, mother, employee, student, friend, daughter, sister, aunt and I'm sure there are roles I haven't listed. I tried to be everything to everybody.

One night after a shower, I discovered a painful lump on my left breast. I am the sort of person who gets mammograms regularly and I try to be as health conscience as possible. I was healthy as a horse or so I thought, not even coming down with a cold in several years.

I made an appointment to see my gynecologist. Since I had been troubled with a cyst on my breast since I was a teen, I didn't think much of it. There was just a niggling feeling that something might be wrong because of the pain associated with this latest cyst. There was no history of breast cancer in my family and cancer wasn't painful, right? My gynecologist referred me to a Surgeon. The Surgeon did a biopsy with a needle that I can remember thinking that it would have been better suited for a horse than a human. The waiting was excruciating. All sorts of scenarios, mostly bad, went through my mind.

A few days or so later, I went back to the Surgeon's office for the results of the biopsy. I went alone, as I told no one but my husband what was going on. The Surgeon set me down and told me I had stage three, triple negative breast cancer. I can barely remember what was said after those words. I had a major melt down.

When I heard the words "You have breast cancer," it was akin to, in my mind, being given a death sentence. The Surgeon asked me if I wanted to call someone to pick me up, but I pulled myself together and drove home in a daze. I called work and told them I would not be back that day. I sat down on the side of my bed and asked myself "Why was this happening?" How was I going to tell my husband and 15 year old daughter that I had breast cancer?" I knew for both their sakes that I had to seem as upbeat as possible. The realization that my time on earth might be up was indescribable. It was hard to come to that realization but through the grace of God, I did. Coming to this realization was a slow process and it happened gradually.

When my husband and my daughter got home, I set them down together and told them about the diagnosis, being as optimistic and upbeat as I possibly could. My husband is a laid back and positive person. He asked a few questions but did not seem overly concerned. My daughter was a shy, sensitive teen. She didn't ask any questions as I can remember but went into her room and closed the door. Looking back, I'm sure they were both as devastated as I. I didn't know how to process it, and I'm pretty sure they did not either.

Having always been a spiritual person but not necessarily a religious person, I asked God for guidance through this dilemma. A few days later, after much prayer, talking to my family, talking to my friends, doing research and going to an Oncologist, I decided to have a lumpectomy. After recovery from the surgery, I went back to work. When it was time for chemo, I took my lunch hour at the end of the day on the Fridays that I had chemo. During the chemotherapy, I lost weight, had no energy, no appetite, and experienced nausea. My hair, eyebrows, and eyelashes fell out, and my nails became yellow and thick. When I was brave enough to look in the mirror at myself, I looked like someone who had barely survived the nuclear holocaust!

During this time, all household duties including laundry, grocery shopping, meals etc. Were done by my husband and daughter. They both were amazing in how they tried to make things as normal as possible. I was like a zombie. I stayed in bed on Saturdays and Sundays after Chemo, but got up Monday mornings to drag into work.

Eventually some semblance of health returned and I had Radiation. I did the Friday afternoon Radiation thing as I had done with the Chemo and continued to work. The Radiation did not affect me as badly as the Chemo. I know God surely got me thru because I don't remember a lot of details about this part of the Journey, especially the Chemo. On the last follow-up visit to the Oncologist, I was pronounced cancer-free. It seemed that all the prayers I solicited and sent up had been answered. I continued my very stressful job and tried to continue my life as though nothing had happened. I made no changes in my lifestyle.

Fast forward and it is now 2004. I have continued the lifestyle I had perpetuated into an art form. My mantra was work like I'm possessed at work, work like I'm possessed at home, and do whatever was asked of me; take no time for myself and put everything and everybody ahead of myself. Well, one morning as I was getting ready for work, I don't know why, but my hand wandered to the incision line of my lumpectomy. I knew there was scar tissue associated with my lumpectomy but what I felt was different. I called the Surgeon for an appointment, praying I was just feeling scar tissue. I knew in my heart the cancer was back, but kept telling myself this wasn't happening again. Sure enough after a sonogram was done, the Surgeon confirmed the cancer was back. It was growing along the incision line where I had the Lumpectomy. I was beside myself. I don't think I heard a word the Doctor said because I had resigned myself to death.

I told my husband and daughter that I had breast cancer again and I don't even remember their reaction because I was crushed. When I finally stopped having my pity party and decided I didn't want to die without putting up a fight, I contacted the Oncologist to see what my options were. I went to an Oncologist at UNC-Chapel Hill Hospital for a second opinion. I decided on mastectomy for my left breast. It was not an easy decision. It is very traumatic losing a part of your body. The emotions associated with losing a part of your body that is associated so closely with a woman's worth are inexpressible. I chose not to have reconstructive surgery. I believe I chose life over a body part I can live without. The lymph nodes taken out at the time of the Mastectomy showed that the cancer had not spread.

My husband changed my bandaging. He also administered the anti-nausea medication that had to be injected and helped me with the drain apparatus. I could not look at myself, much less touch where my breast used to be for a long time, but eventually got used to not having a breast. My family and friends tried to make things as normal as possible for me. To say the second time around was tough is an understatement. I had Chemotherapy, again. The treatment this time did not physically affect me as severely. I had physical therapy to regain mobility in my arm. I had counseling from an excellent councilor. I had counseling because I wanted to be whole mentally, as well as physically.

I experienced an epiphany. This time during the process of surgery and healing, I knew I didn't want to continue on the life path I was on. I wanted things to change so that I could enjoy life and not just go thru the motions of living it as I believe I had been doing. The Chemo left me with nerve damage which limited a lot of the physical things I could do. I knew I could not go back to the stressful career I had. So I asked God to give me the strength to make changes in my life. I quit my stressful job and stepped out on Faith. Quitting my job was not the only change I made. I drank more water, ate more fruits and vegetables, exercised, meditated and the word "No" became a prominent part of my vocabulary.

Being a master of "stretching a dollar until it hollered," we got by on what my husband earned. For the first time in my life, I became a full time wife and mother. But somehow I felt something was missing. So I did some temporary jobs and did some substitute teaching. I finished the requirements I needed to get my BS degree in Business Management, but still felt vaguely dissatisfied.

I decided I wanted to give back and help in the fight against breast cancer. So I went to the local hospital and took training to be a volunteer. I volunteered at the Cancer Registry at our local hospital. It felt so good to be a soldier in the fight against this insidious disease!

My daughter was now getting ready to go to college and I felt guilty about not having much money to contribute to her dream. I had been in the workforce 30 years and felt somewhat lost, not working full time. I found cancer to be stressful monetarily, as well as mentally and physically. So I made up my mind to find something I could do a few days a week for a few hours a day so that my family could have a better cash flow and I could once again feel like a contributing member of society.

I answered an ad for receptionist at a local TV station and got the job! My wonderful, "no one day is like another," 4 1/2 hours a day job at the station and my volunteering were so satisfying! To this day, I continue to volunteer and work my part-time job.

I am so grateful for a second chance at the fulfilling life God has meant for all of us to have. Without God, my family, friends and strategic angels who I met along this journey, I know I would not be relaying this story to you. The path my journey has taken now is one of discovery, an affirmation. I do things that sooth my soul, I pray without ceasing, fight negative thoughts, and find time to go outside myself to help, as well as witness to others.

I look at my journey as a wakeup call God gave me to live life to the fullest and be the best me possible. If I have learned anything from this journey, it is that balance is the most important component of life. You must make time for God and all the things that are truly important on this journey.

Life is such a beautiful gift and so fleeting! We need to submit to God's will and savor every moment God gives us. Although the road has been tough at times as the old Negro Spiritual says "I Wouldn't Take Anything for My Journey Now".

Thank you for letting me share my musings with you. May God bless you and if you are on any sort of journey, keep fighting the good fight!

Sarah Parker

Age: 62
Georgia
30 Year Survivor/Thriver

ABOUT THE AUTHOR

Sarah Parker is a vibrant 62 year old senior who retired in 2007 from the State of Georgia with 30 years of faithful service. My son, Yadrick, Sr. is now a wonderful 43 year old father and grandfather. Oh, YES, I am a proud grandmother of two, a 25 year granddaughter, Trishawn Monee and an 18 year old grandson, Yadrick, Jr.). And...I am a proud and SEXY great-grandmother of beautiful, twin great-grandsons, Jacob Isaiah and Jacobi Elijah. I enjoy traveling around the world and just enjoying life and continue to speak to others who have been diagnosed with breast cancer. I will be enrolling in college to further my education and to broaden my horizon.....I LOVE LIFE!!

Chapter 8

Life does not end with CANCER!

By

Sarah Parker

My journey began in March 1984 when I was at the age of 32. After doing a breast exam, I discovered an unusual dimple under my right breast. I had remembered the seven warning signs and this was one of them. This occurrence was on the weekend, so I was nervous having to wait until Monday morning when I could call my doctor.

I went in for an exam and was scheduled for a biopsy the following week. After the biopsy and after receiving the results, I was told that it was cancer and that I would need to have a mastectomy. I was horrified out of my wits and scared! I sought two more opinions and was told the same thing.

You see, I considered myself a young, 32 year old, beautiful, youthful and sexy female. The only thing I thought about was that they wanted to remove my breast. I thought I would no longer be sexy anymore and appealing; I did not think that I might die! After calming down and realizing what was happening, I came to my senses and said "Girl, you have a son to raise." He was only 13 at the time.

So in July 1984, I had the mastectomy and began chemotherapy for 6 six months. That was the worst ordeal I had ever experienced in my life...beginning with the nausea! My hair falling out! My being tired; My nails turning black and even sores in my mouth!! Remember, this was 1984 and the medications were very severe and harsh. My veins began to dissolve and burn out from the IV after taking so much medicine. I was getting ready to have a port put in because my veins were gone in my right arm and I could not take the IV in my left arm because some of lymph nodes were removed.

Most people lose weight during these treatments (90%). Of course, I was in the 10% range and I gained five pounds just about every treatment. Now that was even more depressing!

When my hair began to come out (after the first treatment), I just decided to comb it all out and just be bald headed. It was scary and humiliating to me and my son. I thought my son was okay with it. I was not, but eventually I got used to it and I would not wear my wigs on the weekend; just when I went to work. So I started buying wigs every payday. I would come back from lunch as somebody new☺.

I elected not to get reconstruction surgery because I thought it might happen to my other breast so I said I would wait and see. But it did not happen and I still decided not to get reconstruction because I did not want to get cut on again.

During this journey, I received a visit from a Reach to Recovery volunteer and was not pleased at all with the volunteer. She was a Black female and very disillusioned about life because her life had stopped! She stated that she had stopped dating and having fun. I knew that was not for me – a happy person. I felt sorry for her and decided that I wanted to be a different type volunteer.

I went to classes and became a volunteer ~~one~~ because I felt that my life was not ending there Towards the end of my treatments, I decided that I did not want to continue chemo because I would get sick when I entered the doctors' building. ~~so~~ One of my co-workers started taking me and I completed chemo.

After treatment, the doctors stated that there could be a five-year reoccurrence. Of course, during those first - five years, I was just nervous about the results from my mammogram. But they came back clear… thank the Lord. You see, God is good all the time and I have and had faith. I know now that "no weapon formed against me shall prosper." I started running or walking for breast cancer awareness and became an advocate by speaking to friends and others who were going through this ordeal. I have met some awesome people along the way, including Paula Broadnax.

I speak out all the time about my journey because without the support of family, friends, co-workers; and of course, GOD...I don't think I would be here mentally. I did seek psychotherapy because I was having problems adjusting to having only one breast. I thought my sexuality was gone; but I overcame that.

During my time as a volunteer, I enjoyed being able to talk to the patients and answer questions about their concerns and worries, and letting them know that life does not end here...it gets better!

This journey has taught me to "Live your life to the fullest, because tomorrow is not promised to us; to love one another and be kind and thoughtful to others; say nice things and give compliments because you never know what your fellow man is going through." This journey also brought my faith in God to a higher level and a better understanding life. I believe this journey has made me a wholesome individual and made me more aware of my body and health.

I now attend the Helene S. Mills Senior Center where I take a nutrition class; do cardio, line dancing, and water aerobics for my physical health. It is also a great social outlet which keeps me active. I have met all kinds of people. So, yes ...this journey has not always been cheerful, but I'm still standing.

Life does not end with CANCER!

Dovetta Taylor

Age: 51
Maryland
5 Year Survivor/Thriver

ABOUT THE AUTHOR

Dovetta Taylor is the single mother of two adult children. She resides in Baltimore, Maryland. Dovetta has been employed for 17 years as a school bus attendant for a local school system. As such, she is a blessing in helping children (some with special physical needs, some with emotional and developmental needs) being transported to and from school.

She also serves at her local church sharing her culinary expertise by contributing meals, soups and cookies at events. Dovetta has become proactive with her health during and since her recovery by becoming a vegetarian and keeping physically active— and in so doing has lost a significant amount of weight and has reduced the amount of prescription medication she once required. While on this journey, she looks forward to moving deeper into the area of cooking/nutrition and possibly becoming an entrepreneur by opening up her own café and educating others on healthy eating and healthy living.

Chapter 9

A FUNNY THING HAPPENED ON THE LIGHT RAIL

by

Dovetta Taylor

My name is Dovetta. Friends and family call me Doe. I don't know how to start or where to start. I don't even know if my story is worth sharing; but for some reason, I was asked to share. So where do I begin??

I live in Baltimore City and work for the Baltimore County Public Schools (BCPS) System as a bus attendant. I love my job! It allows me to meet a bevy of parents and students.

I'm a single parent. My children are grown, living in other states (as it should be, in my opinion). I have no pets, even though people think I should. But I feel it is not fair to the pet to be cooped up while I'm at work--that's just me. I have a vast collection of cookbooks and cooking clippings. They are not for show. I really use a lot of them and have been known to have great dinners and good company. But enough chatting—let me get back to thinking about what I can say about my experience after I was told I had breast cancer.

I was on spring break, and had already set up an appointment to have my mammogram done like I do each and every year. That was April 6, 2009. A few days later on April 8, 2009, I received a letter saying that "Your *Diagnostic Mammogram performed on 4/06/2009 shows a suspicious area that needs further evaluation.*" So I dismissed it as something I would take care of when I went back to work, not really paying attention, and not thinking that anything was wrong. I have gotten one of these notices before, and it was just a blip--except this time it was not a blip!

I was leaving a counselor's office one night as I was having a session for some issues in my life. Up the street from where the office was located was a Super Fresh Market. Now, when I tell this story to people, I use a timeframe context because this happened so fast and my world changed from Harford Road to Belair Road.

Back to the-market (Side note: I find supermarket shopping therapeutic, so I have no issues staying in a store for two hours, just walking up and down aisles.) So, I'm walking the aisles of the store, picking up some things to take home when my cell phone rang. It was the radiology doctor indicating they saw something and just wanted me to come back in so they could take a look at it. I was really only half listening and wondering should I buy these really great paper plates that were going to be discontinued. I asked her what she thought it was and she said that it might not be anything major. They just needed to make sure it was not carcinoma in situ. I asked "what was that?" The sound of her voice made it seem like nothing urgent or a big deal. So, I took it as such and figured when I returned to work I would go back and have someone look at it. The place I went for mammograms was close to where I worked.

I ended the call and headed to the next aisle. Just when I'm turning the corner to the next aisle, my phone rings again! "Dovetta! This is Dr. Rivera at GYN. Who told you to go get a mammogram?" I'm in full alert and paying attention now. I said. "I do this every year." He said, "I don't think I want you doing this alone." I was like—"Hold up, what is going on??" The radiology doctor just called and made it seem like it was not big deal. He said I might have carcinoma in situ. I inquired "What is it?" He said, "Small cluster inside your breast tissue contained to one area." I stopped walking and listened, still trying to figure out what he was saying. He said, "I have a doctor who I want you to see. Her name is Dr. Fernandez. I was like ok--thinking I would just have to go to his office to pick up a referral. But that was on the Harford Road side.

I left the store confused and with my small bag of groceries and no paper plates. I went across the street to the 19 bus stop to wait for the bus, still wondering what was going on. The bus came. I went to the next stop to take the 55 bus. As I stood at the stop, I was slightly wondering what was going on to make Dr. Rivera call. The bus came. The next stop was on Belair Road. My phone rang again JUST AS I WAS ABOUT TO STEP OFF THE BUS. "Hi, Ms. Taylor. This is blank (did not hear her full name) from Dr. Fernandez's office. We have an appointment for you to come into the office to see the doctor." What appointment? Who is this doctor? Is she at the breast center? "Who is Dr. Fernandez and who made the appointment?" I asked. "Dr. Rivera made your appointment to come to be seen," was the reply. "What is the breast center?" I asked. The response was "it is where the doctors deal with women who may have breast cancer?" I was in disbelief! I called my friend Debbie and said, "I guess they think I may have cancer!"

A Funny thing happened on the Light Rail...

The week I found out was the most stressful work week for me. I had just returned from a two-day training session in Timonium, Md. It was the last day, and I was riding the light rail home. I'm sitting on the train listening to a guy talk about why orange soda should be the only soda people drink, when my phone rang. It was Nurse Carol from the Breast Center calling to tell me about the results from all of the tests. She said that the test came back that I did have cancer. She wanted to go into more detail, but I said I was not home and could I call her back later when I get home. I was trying not to cry, and hang on until I got home. I called my daughter Basha when I got settled to do a three way call so she could hear what I was not hearing. I don't think either of us truly heard what was said.

Moving Through it All...

I have never had so many mammograms, CT scans, PT scans, MRIs, and other tests and doctor visits in my life! Getting poked, prodded--and not in the good way. So many doctors and nurses looking at me and checking me out--asking if I smoked or was pregnant, which was NO to both questions. Being asked if I had a living will at each and every appointment was odd. Being under anesthesia more than I have ever been, and waking up in the middle of one procedure, (which was funny--I heard the doctor asking the nurse how did she know what he did on vacation. Well I busted out laughing. He said "Dovetta, are you awake?" I said "yes!" They must have put me back to sleep. LOL!) I would get medication once or twice every three years. When I look back, all I can say is "thank God for insurance, and people who help when insurance won't cover certain things."

The thing that really got me was the surgeries and how fast each one happened, from the mastectomy, port, and reconstruction, to nipple replacement. I was just moving through it all. People kept asking me how I felt and I had no answer, I just wanted it all to stop. It was very overwhelming and I could not do some things. If I had to go somewhere, it took me two hours to get dressed, and please, don't let there be a change of plans; that was another hour added. There was a lot to do. Trying to make sure the tube sticking out my side was well covered and protected even from me. Visiting nurses; in and out of the hospital; making sure my temperature stayed under 100. Keeping my doctors on speed dial!

Trying to keep all those appointments straight and I did forget a few. And then there were those chemo treatments. the periodic muscle cramping I now get from chemo and the brain fog. It was crazy to be working while taking chemo, trying to staying upbeat and happy, when I just wanted to curl up and cry. Then there was losing my hair and it coming back with a lot more gray--just a roller coaster of emotions that never fully get dealt with. Wow--It was a lot!

Single when all this happened, I still was not at the processing point of what was really going on with me. I mean I did not smoke, work with chemicals, or eat certain meats. So to this day, I still try to process--how did it happen? Most of all, I was concerned about who would take care of me. I'm single, so who would help me? I did not know how to do this. I don't have a husband or boyfriend to help me out. I would later learn from others that this may have been a good thing. What was I going to do??

From the time the diagnosis was truly confirmed, God set wheels in motion!   There is a scripture in Psalm 68:5-6a which states "Father to the fatherless, a defender of widows, is God in His holy dwelling. God sets the lonely in families." This was what made me realize God does love and care for me. It opened the door for a lot of care from people I knew and did not know. Getting rides to appointments, people sitting with me during chemo, taking me in the early mornings to surgeries, sitting and praying for and with me, stopping to see me at chemo, staying with me after surgery. The doctors and nurses of Franklin Square and St. Joseph's Hospital were kind and helpful to me. Organizations that are too many to mention, help in amazing ways, with services I did not know existed. Being single does not stop illness from coming your way, just like being single does not make you less of a person. God will provide if you just ask Him to help. Yes, it's scary not knowing who you can depend on for help, but casting pride aside will open doors for you, provide the help and bless you beyond measure.

From the time of going to the doctor for the first appointment or to just make me laugh, God had someone for me. I had family, my daughter Basha and son Xavier, my mother Evelyn Taylor, church family River of Life Christian Center, some of the ladies from TWI (The Women Institute) people from my job--many, many, many people to thank who helped in some way. From helping me find a place to live before I started chemo, to moving. There was an abundance of blessings. There were so many people, and even after all the appointments and surgeries and there are still people helping me. God knows who we need and when we need them, if we just lean on Him. I have learned that I am not alone!!

What Now?...

I'm not climbing mountains or starting a foundation. I know some people have these life changing epiphanies. I'm just getting my feet back on the ground. The doctors' appointments are less than before. I still have the port flushes every eight weeks. I'm still seeing my breast doctor and oncology doctor. I'm still having my mammograms each spring or as the doctors feel I need them. I just had a biopsy done this year because of something they saw in the sonogram. As of this writing, they just want to keep an eye on it. Other than that, I feel like myself more each day. The fog has been lifted and I keep moving forward.

I will have done two Dirty Girl Mud Runs--one in 2013 and an upcoming one in 2014. I volunteer with the Baltimore Free Store. I've been an extra in a few church plays. I'm back to cooking and baking and having dinners from time to time. And now I have been trying to decide what is next for me in life. But, for now I laugh, smile, and hang out with people who make me happy. And that's just fine.

Mia Williams

Age: 49

Maryland
6 Year Survivor/Thriver

ABOUT THE AUTHOR

Mia Curtis Williams is an outgoing, divorced mother of two young sons, ages 8 and 11. She has worked as an Administrator for Johns Hopkins University and recently held a position in local government. Ms. Williams has an entrepreneurial spirit and owns a gift basket business which allows her to create beautiful, customized baskets for her clients. She plans on pursuing more creative endeavors and traveling the world. She is a six year Cancer overcomer, residing in Baltimore County, Maryland.

Chapter 10

My New Level of Faith

By

Mia Williams

On September 8, 2008, I received a phone call that changed my life in a way I would never have imagined. Every concern or problem I had prior to that moment faded to black instantaneously.

A few weeks prior, I had my annual mammogram and received a letter in the mail informing me that my results were not normal and that I should schedule an appointment for another one. I scheduled the appointment and went to the Breast Center at Johns Hopkins where they performed a more intense screening that looked more closely at the calcifications in my right breast. I was told that they were confident that the calcifications were benign. I was given the option to either have a biopsy or follow up in six months.

When I asked how confident they were that they were benign, they said "very confident," but they couldn't give me anything in writing. The radiologist showed me my films, which showed a large number of tiny sand-sized dots in my right breast. I decided to go for the biopsy since they couldn't guarantee that it was benign -- after all, six months is a long time to wait if they were wrong!

About a week later, I returned to the Breast Center for a stereotactic biopsy where they placed tiny metal markers where they take tissue, so that they know where they took it from. I was really having the biopsy done to confirm that the calcifications were benign, as they had said.

During the procedure, the radiologist told me that he was confident this was benign which helped while I underwent this uncomfortable procedure. I left feeling confident. I would wait for the results and try not to worry. I was shown the film of my breast which showed the tiny dots all throughout my breast.

So, on September 8th, I was sitting at work at my desk and received a phone call from my mother. She said that Dr. Eisenberg, the Radiologist, had called and left a message for me to call him. She gave me the number. I was surprised that he had called himself and hadn't had a nurse from the office call me to let me know my results were fine. I felt nervous immediately and I could tell that my mother was concerned by her voice.

I called Dr. Eisenberg back, but he was on the phone. I asked to hold. He got on the phone and said that he was sorry to tell me that the result of my biopsy was that the calcifications were malignant. It was DCIS (Ductal Carcinoma In Sutu). He actually said, "If you are going to get cancer, this is the kind you want to get. It is very early and hasn't spread to the breast tissue." He said he was surprised because he really thought it was benign. He told me to schedule an appointment with the Breast Center. I was numb and couldn't really wrap my brain around what he had told me.

To be honest, everything felt surreal, as if it couldn't possibly be happening. So much so that I called the doctor back and told him there must be some mistake. I explained that my last name was Williams, which is common and that he must have had my results mixed up with another Williams. He assured me that he always double checked before calling patients and that I was the right Mia Williams. I hung up, stunned. I really don't remember leaving and getting into my car.

I do remember calling my mom and telling her what the doctor had said. I remember hearing the words coming out of my mouth and still not believing that it was happening. Fear gripped me almost immediately.

This was even more devastating because my father was receiving chemotherapy for bladder cancer and my mom was going with him for his treatments. I had just separated from my husband in April. My two young sons, ages two and five, were living with my parents.

So the fight began. I had an appointment with the surgeon fairly quickly. I was stunned when she told me I would need a mastectomy, almost matter of factly. Neither my Mom, nor I, was prepared for that. I thought I would need a lumpectomy. I thought, early Stage One and I need a mastectomy! That can't be! I even suggested that they just "scoop" out the tissue where the spots were. That was not an option, I was told. We left the appointment with our heads spinning. My Mom was not happy about the way the doctor was nonchalant about delivering such news.

We made an appointment to come back and discuss things in greater detail. I did my research before my next meeting with the doctor and learned that there were instances when you could keep your areola and nipple, which made for a more natural look. The "good" news according to the surgeon was that I could keep my nipple and areola. The plastic surgeon there told me that I would come out of surgery with an "A" cup and not be totally flat. They began moving and working on scheduling my surgery quickly. They gave me a date in early October, but I wanted a second opinion.

I decided three things immediately… I was going to fight with all I had. I was going to be strong in my faith and keep a positive outlook and I was only telling people who were strong in their faith and would speak life to my situation and not death. **AND** I was not going to allow my kids to be traumatized by this or try to explain the diagnosis.

I scheduled an appointment at Mercy Medical Center and met with Dr. Beda for a second opinion. My mom and I met with her together. She spent a long time taking my family history of cancer, and unlike many doctors, she was not dismissive of the high incidence of cancer in my family just because it wasn't my mother or grandmother. She talked to me in her office first, and then examined me, which was another plus. She then confirmed that she agreed that I should have had a mastectomy; **HOWEVER**, keeping my areola and nipple would not be possible because small cells could have been passed to them during my biopsy.

I truly expected that was what made me decide to not have my surgery at Johns Hopkins and go to Mercy. I wanted a doctor who would be taking all precautions in order to save my life with the highest likelihood for a positive outcome. I called Hopkins and cancelled my surgery. They were not very happy because they had been working on coordinating everyone needed from the anesthesiologist, to the surgeon, the Operating Room, etc.; but I was sure that I was making the right decision. The bonus was that Dr. Bedi was formerly at Hopkins and had gone to Mercy, so I was getting a top notch surgeon, but with more wisdom.

So, my mastectomy with Dr. Bedi was scheduled for November 5, 2008. It was now October and I was concerned that it was too far away. As soon as I heard the diagnosis, I wanted it out of me...immediately. She assured me that it was fine and not too far away. Now I had to wrap my mind around the thought of losing my breast. Having it done was a no brainer, if it would save my life and allowed me to live to see my sons grow into manhood, I was doing it. Yet, I had the vision of them literally cutting off my breast. I remember my great grandmother had breast cancer and she was flat on the side of her surgery with a scar. This was back in the 70's, but I still thought about what I would look like, and how it would affect me as far as meeting someone who would want me with only one breast.

I had to meet with my plastic surgeon at Mercy, Dr. Chang, to discuss what type of reconstruction I wanted (an implant or the flap, where they take muscle from your back and fat from your stomach) and what size I would get. There were so much research to do and decisions to make. I decided that I would begin the reconstructive surgery during my surgery and I would have an implant. Dr. Chang said I would be an "A" cup after surgery and that he would put a little saline in my expander so that I wasn't totally flat.

I didn't realize at the time that I would have a long close relationship with these doctors and that they would forever be a big part of my "new normal." The comforting part of this was that Dr. Bedi told me that surgery would most likely be the cure for my cancer and that I would most likely not need Chemo or Radiation. This was a great source of comfort for me, but I was still battling thoughts of "what if "day and night. From the moment I was told the result of my biopsy, FEAR gripped me.

Although I am a Christian who believes in the power of prayer and healing, I had never been faced with such a challenge as this and I was terrified. I used to lay wide awake at night, praying and battling negative thoughts that the devil was constantly trying to plant in my mind. My family history with cancer didn't help the situation either. When they say "the mind is the battlefield" that statement became truer than I had ever realized. I was in a full Battle...just like that!

I cannot say how fortunate I am to have a family that prays. My Mother has always been calm and reassuring. I knew that this must have been extremely difficult for her to have her husband and only child fighting this disease at the same time. I really can't imagine. Yet my Mom was there with both of us, every step of the way, being supportive. My father was also very supportive and he could relate to me because he was going through the same thing. He could talk to me firsthand about the chemo and the after affects. I will always remember the day when I told him that I was concerned about losing a breast and how it would affect my future. I was going through a divorce and wondered how a man would react to my being a breast cancer survivor who had a mastectomy. My father said that anyone who let that affect how they felt about me, didn't deserve me and wasn't the one for me –Period! He was absolutely right, of course.

On November 5th, I had to be at the hospital very early in the morning. I believe it was 5 or 6 a.m. I had explained to my kids that I was going to the hospital and would be staying overnight and that they would have to be gentle with me when I came home. I told them I wouldn't be able to pick them up when I came home. I never told them what I was diagnosed with because they were so young and wouldn't understand. Along with my mother, my good friend, Dawn came to the hospital with me. My father was taking care of my kids for the day. We waited in the day surgery waiting room and I was in pretty good spirits, considering. I was all prayed up by family and friends and going to be a trooper.

I remember them calling me back, starting my IV, which I have always hated since I have tiny veins, and then my mom and Dawn coming back with me. Everyone was extremely nice to me in the surgical department. I think partially because I was younger than typical patients (and I looked younger than I was). It was probably when the Anesthesiologist came to talk to me and they put the cap over my hair, that I suddenly became overwhelmed with fear. The reality of it all just hit me. I was losing my breast and I would never be the same after I came out of the Operating Room.

My Mom and Dawn prayed with me and assured me everything was going to be fine. I remember Dr. Bedi came and checked on me and told me she would see me in the O.R. I remember going into the O.R .and it being FREEZING, as all Operating Rooms are. I was really scared and they got me situated with both my arms out to the side. I was relieved when the Anesthesiologist said he would put something in my IV to relax me because I was ready to be knocked out. The truth was that at times like that, it is truly you and the Lord going in together and you must trust Him.

I remember waking up in the recovery room after my surgery. I remember my Mom and Dawn coming to see me and being there. It was about eight o'clock in the evening, but I couldn't believe it was so late. It seemed like I had just gone in. I was extremely hungry because I hadn't eaten since the night before and I remember asking if I could have some crackers or something to eat. I remember having some crackers and juice very slowly, because they didn't want me to get sick from the anesthesia. They were getting ready to transport me to my room and soon my Mom and Dawn were kissing me goodbye. I brought my MP3 player loaded with Christian music with me to the hospital to comfort me the night of my surgery. I didn't know how I was going to feel physically or emotionally.

I was in my room resting comfortably. I wasn't in any pain. Really groggy at first, but as the night went on, I called the nurse to help me get to the bathroom a couple times, and then decided I could do it myself. I got- my Praise and Worship Music and I praised the Lord that night, for bringing me through the surgery and for being with me. He was with me and that was the time that people talk about when it is just you and God. I really understood it that night. I said that I would praise Him even in the midst of the trial and I did just that on that night at Mercy Medical Center. I cried and praised the Lord and I felt surprisingly strong. I played "Grateful" by Hezekiah Walker and "Total Praise" by Richard Smallwood many times.

The next day, the doctor came to check on me and I was feeling just fine. No pain because I had this ball that was administering medication to my breast. I couldn't believe how good I felt. He asked if I had looked at my incision. I answered, "No, I wasn't ready to look at it yet." I could tell though that I wasn't flat as a pancake, as I had expected. He said I could go home and that a nurse would come to check on me at home. I still couldn't believe that they send people home the day after a mastectomy, but they surely did. I went home the next evening. I was released around five p.m.

The mastectomy was hands down the easiest part of the entire ordeal. Now, the showering with the medicine ball in a bag was quirk, but my mom stood outside of the shower and held the bag for me. The nurse came to my home to check on me a couple of times. Getting the expander filled every two weeks was hands down the most painful part. Initially, it was easy because I didn't feel it, but the more saline that was added, the more it stretched your skin to make room for the implant, and it was like having a brick in your chest. It was very painful. I had to go back after one visit to have them take some of the saline out because I couldn't take the pain.

I waited to get the call from Dr. Bedi to confirm that I would not need to have chemo or radiation. We had to wait for the results from the lab examining the tissue. I remember exactly when she called. It was a cold night in late November. I couldn't drive yet and my Mom drove me to K-Mart to pick something up. I was walking in the store when the phone rang and it was her. She said that everything was early Stage One and chemo and radiation were off the table. Not needed. I think I screamed in K-Mart that night. I was so very happy and thankful. I ran to the car to tell my Mom the good news. What a relief!!! Or so I thought.

At my follow-up appointment, Dr. Bedi informed me that I needed to make an appointment with an Oncologist. I quickly questioned why and she explained that he is the one who prescribes the Tamoxifen that I would have to take for the next five years. It cuts the risk of cancer in the other breast by 50% when taken daily for five years. So, I scheduled the appointment with Dr. Riseberg at Mercy. I had my faithful Mom in tow with me of course. What I thought would just be a routine appointment to get my prescription and explain everything about Tamoxifen, turned out to be more than I expected.

First, we discussed the side effects of Tamoxifen, which include an increase risk for blood clots, risk for uterine cancer, hot flashes and other menopausal symptoms including mood swings!! I was really not comfortable with the side effects, especially the risk for uterine cancer. He explained that the group which this occurred in was older women 70 years old and over, not my age group. Then he drops a bomb on me telling me he recommended I should do it! I said "Oh no!" Dr, Bedi told me chemo and radiation were not needed and that my surgery was my cure... He said that it was very early stage; however, the "tumors" were estrogen/progesterone receptive. He said it was more like an assurance that if there were any lingering cells, they would be killed. I was extremely upset and so was my Mom. I knew Dr. Riseberg very well now and really liked him a lot but that day he was a bit "matter of fact" too. My Mom was not happy either. We both knew that we would get a second opinion about the chemo. I looked at the top hospitals in cancer. The number one hospital listed was Anderson in Texas, Memorial Sloan-Kettering in New York, and Hopkins was number three at the time.

On Friday, March 6th, two days after my oldest son's 6th birthday, we headed to New York for my appointment at Memorial Sloan Kettering Hospital in Manhattan. When I say "we," I mean the whole crew --my parents, my kids and me. I decided that if I was going to my favorite place, we were going to make a trip of it, squeeze some fun out of it. I lived in New York (Queens) and Northern New Jersey (Hackensack) and although I used to hang out in New York often, I never get tired of going back or have been anywhere as exciting. My oncologist fully supported my going to Memorial Sloan-Kettering for a second opinion.

So, my father watched the kids while my Mom and I went to my appointment. The purpose of the visit was to determine if I really needed to do the chemo that was recommended by my oncologist in Maryland or not. I have nothing but excellent things to say about Memorial Sloan-Kettering Hospital. They handled everything like top notch professionals. From the help I received when I first called to let them know I wanted to make the appointment, getting my slides and medical records to them, and then the way they treated me upon my arrival was just great.

The doctor and her resident were awesome. They were very thorough and took their time with me, and she was very caring with me. She listened well and I feel she really looked at the whole picture of me and my life. At the end of the visit, she said that given my young age, she would recommend that I do the chemo as well. The difference came when she recommended a different drug combination from my Maryland oncologist. She recommended Taxol only, vs. Taxol and Carboplatin. She said this would be easier on me but the studies had shown to have the same results. She also told me not to shave my head because there was a 50/50 chance that I would not lose all of my hair and go bald. It wasn't what I wanted to hear, but I was so glad I went. I truly believe that the Lord sent me to Memorial Sloan-Kettering and because of it; I received an easier round of drugs which provided me the same excellent results as the more taxing drugs. This is where going for second opinions at top notch facilities is ever so worth it. Everyone should get a second opinion, period!

I am not knocking my doctors at Mercy in any way whatsoever. They simply treated my stage with the certain combinations that they always had. It wasn't until a couple of years after my chemo, that I learned that I was the first patient with my diagnosis that they treated with Taxol only. My oncologist, whom I have since grown to like very much and befriended, told me that my name comes up in meetings now because I was the first, and now they use that treatment for other patients. He always keeps me abreast of what they are talking about at the conferences that he goes to when I have an appointment with him. I really appreciate that he treats me with respect, values my thoughts and opinion, and shares the new information he learns. He even recommended a vacation spot that I really enjoy going to with my family

The day we were in New York, my father was waiting to hear from his oncologist to find out the results of his labs concerning his treatment for bladder cancer. He was a little anxious waiting for the call. He received the call after my appointment when we were in the room. He received a good report. We were happy that day. Even though I would have to do the chemo, I was thankful for the different approach. We relaxed and then went to dinner at one of my old favorites, Dallas Barbeque. My parents and kids had never been there. Just basic food, chicken, cornbread and vegetables, but they give you a lot of food. We had a good time. The next day, we ordered breakfast in our room and my stepsister and nephew came to the hotel. We all went to FAO Schwartz for an outing. The kids had a great time and left happy, of course. Soon after that, we headed back to the hotel, got the car and headed back to Maryland.

On Wednesday of the next week, I had a port placed in my chest for the chemo. I was TERRIFIED of the thought of having a catheter placed in my jugular vein. The possibility of a blood clot forming in it almost put me in a panic. I literally could not sleep the night I got my port. I know I wore my parents out during those first days. I was totally gripped with fear. I insisted they call me from the phone downstairs to check on me to make sure I was okay because I was scared a blood clot would form in my catheter and they would not know it. I slept propped up with pillows because I was scared to lie down. I had this foreign object that clearly protruded out of my chest and you could see the vein the catheter was in too. It just felt uncomfortable, especially at first. If turned my neck a certain way, it felt uncomfortable as well. It kind of makes me cringe thinking about it now.

But, I battled all the fears I had with the Word of God. My aunt sent me this little book/pamphlet published by a good friend of hers who is in Ministry called "Confessions for Health" by Pastor Gwendolyn Young. She also gave me the CD to play in my car. That little book helped me fight fear daily and win. I wore that book out. I have it in my night stand next to my bed. It is taped up and tattered and I still love it and use it.

Exactly one week later after going to New York for my second opinion, on March 13, 2009, I started my first of 13 chemo treatments. Every Friday for 13 weeks! My Mom came to every single one with me and sat with me for the most of the day appointments.

I will never forget my first one though. I had a violently negative reaction to the drug a few minutes after the drug was started. My nurse was Pauline. I liked her instantly. She was nice, but very serious about what she did, because let's face it, Chemotherapy is NO JOKE! Soon after the drug was started, Pauline was looking at me to monitor me and I told her I felt a little sick, like I might vomit. She got me one of those plastic containers for that. Then I started having these violent pains in my stomach and then very quickly starting having very labored breathing. I told her I didn't feel so good.

Then everything happed really fast, I think. I felt my eyes rolling back and felt like I was going to faint. She laid me back, she yelled "I need some help" and about four nurses came running in. My Mom stood up and came to my side, grabbed my hand and started praying immediately. There was a lot of ruckus around me but I felt my Mom's hand the whole time and I could hear her. I didn't know what they were doing, but they stopped the drug, gave me steroids for having a reaction, and called my oncologist to come.

When I opened my eyes and was feeling better, he was sitting down next to me. He asked "Are you feeling better?" and I was. He stayed for a few minutes and then left when I was stable. I don't know how long he had been there. I was ready to go home right then, after resting for a while, Pauline said "okay, we're going to try this again." I was really scared again, but she told me that they had given me some drugs to prevent a reaction and they were going to run the drug slower this time.

Well, it went just fine the second time around. My Mom and I were there until about 8 p.m. that night. The nurses commented, "You gave us a scare" as we were leaving. I was too happy to get home and see my sons that night, and I never wanted to go back there again. I requested Pauline to be my nurse every week and she was, except for one, and that was not a good day. But other than that, it went well.

I was cheerful and positive when I went there. I always tried to be thankful that I wasn't worse than I was. They had an artist come around with different forms of art that you could do. Charcoal, paint, etc... My Mom and I both did it some weeks.

One week, they asked me talk to another patient. She was younger, like me and they wanted her to have chemo, but she was scared and was leaning toward not doing it. She was African American, too. They thought that I might get through to her. So I spoke to her and her Mom. I told her a bit of my story and that I had two young sons and would do anything I had to be around to see them grow up and be around.

I KNOW that God spared me from a lot of the "norms" of chemo. I also believe that He used me to encourage someone and that he will continue to use me in that way. I didn't get sick one time; didn't go bald; my blood work was good every week; so that I never had to skip a week and I worked through all of my chemo, (even though I started to feel tired as it went on). I worked Monday through Thursday, full time. I took Fridays off and went back to work on Monday. I did have neuropathy in my hands and feet and lost my sense of taste for the first three days after the treatments. My hair shed a lot and I just had it cut really short and wore hair pieces. My skin darkened. I had "chemo brain," too — and yes, chemo brain is real! Your memory can definitely be affected. I gained 10 pounds due to the steroids I had to take to prevent another bad reaction, but I was I was so thankful that it wasn't worse because it surely could have been!

My last treatment was on May 29, 2009. I had a little celebration on my birthday, June 7th to celebrate my birthday and my last chemo. I celebrated with a handful of close friends.

I had to do a year of Herceptin after Taxol, which I started on June 5th, but that was easy and didn't have any side effects. I was trying to get back to normal during that year. My neuropathy faded slowly. My taste buds weren't affected and my hair slowly started growing back. My periods had stopped completely, which was fine with me. My last Herceptin treatment was March 12, 2010 and I had my port removed as soon as I could get on my surgeon's schedule which was March 22, 2010.

I cannot even explain how happy I was to get that port removed. It also represented the end of a chapter in my life which was the hardest chapter in my life, but the chapter that taught me how to lean on God fully and absolutely. It also taught me that when I say "I am more than a conqueror," I really am. I am capable of doing things I never thought I could because of the Lord and only because of his Grace and Mercy. How else could I go through this while going through a separation, moving back home with my parents with my two and five year old sons working, going on with life normally so that my kids would not be traumatized, moving into my own place with my kids for the first time ever, finding a new job, getting divorced, and being single again.

I wondered very briefly why this had happened to me -- but why not me? Several people have told me that it is proof that I was used for the Lord's work. People with big challenges like this are being used. I believe He knew that He could use me. I promised that I would let everyone know that it was only Him who brought me through that ordeal.

I didn't want to simply give a chronological account of my experience, because this was my life, for several years. It seems like a blur now. As I shared what I went through, I hope I didn't ever make it sound easy because it wasn't. I have had multiple reconstructive surgeries, too many appointments to recall. I am treated differently whenever I see a doctor due my past experience. They call it your "new normal"; but I have a new normal after my new normal by my ordeal. I just graduated to having a mammogram and living like most women do and waiting to have the results mailed to me. That was a little challenging because for the last five years, I waited until the radiologist read my films, and I left knowing that everything is good. I became accustomed to that. I even contemplated asking if they could read them before I left this last time. But, I waited and received my letter in the mail saying that everything was normal.

My follow-up appointments have become spaced farther as well. So, things have changed now as I am about to approach my 6 sixth year anniversary on September 8, 2014, and they will continue to change for my good.

In addition to raising my sons, I am reviving my basket business, taking courses online toward completing my degree and looking forward to a fulfilling life. My future is bright and full of hope. I tell EVERYONE that it was ONLY the Lord that brought me through it. I do believe the Lord showed me that if I really, really hand it over to him, He will truly do His best and better than I can hope for.

I am thankful for so many things in my life. I have awesome parents who are an immeasurable support in helping me with my sons. I have two beautiful sons who are the reason I do it all and I have a great extended family and friends who bless me in many ways.

But my She-ro is my Mom, Barbara Holmes. She is a quiet boulder of strength. She is sweet, kind, and more patient than most. She has ALWAYS been there for me when I needed her (and even when I thought I didn't). She is honest with me, even if I don't want to hear it, encouraging to me, loving towards me, and supportive of me. She laughs with me, cries with me, and travels with me -- LOL. I am more than blessed to have the privilege to have her as my mother and Mom - Mom to my sons. I know people say it all the time, but I really want to have a spirit like hers when I grow up.

Finally, these words resound in my heart from the night in my hospital room... "I am Grateful for the things that you have done; yes I'm Grateful for the victories we've won. I could go ON and ON and ON...about your works because I'm Grateful just to praise you Lord. Flowing from my heart are the issues of my heart. It's Gratefulness."

I am blessed to be a blessing and I am confident of this, that He who began a good work in me will perform it until the day of Jesus. Be Blessed!

We Survive to Thrive

Closing Thoughts...

WE HAVE SURVIVED TO THRIVE!!

Paula Smith Broadnax

Well, it is now finished and what a phenomenal project this has been for me. I knew that it would be because I was being lead to so many women who had been through a breast cancer journey like me.

One of the things that was so impressive about them was their countenance of spirit and the joy and life that I saw and hear in their faces and in their voices. It was so enjoyable to hear bits of their journey that they would share with me. So, I knew that if they had the opportunity to tell more of their stories, many people could be inspired and encouraged.

Upon approaching many of them, some were ready to re-open themselves to what some was a painful experience (mentally and physically). Others were not at a place of sharing yet. Of course, that was okay because what I know is that we must have moved beyond the pain and other feelings that accompanied the trial.

Those who have shared are on "the other side of through" and are now thriving in their lives. They have embraced the experience and are sharing their testimonies with others in their daily walks and in this awesome book that God has allowed us to compile.

It is our desire that anyone who picks up this book and reads it will know that we all will go through trials. The operative word is THROUGH! It is a journey with an end to it. What matters is how we trek through the experience.

As these writers have shown – there is a NEW BEGINNING (not ending) which comes with love for God, love for one's self, knowing our bodies, seeking assistance, asking questions, taking care of self, surrounding ourselves with positive people and lastly, NEVER GIVING UP.

Finally, if we approach each of life's trial in this manner...we will continue to SURVIVE TO THRIVE!!

Peace, love and blessings to each of you!

For continued encouragement, inspiration and resources to thrive in your life join...

Legacy Creations

create, live and leave a godly legacy for the world!

Our Legacy Creations community was created by Paula Smith Broadnax to inspire others to understand the value of leaving a godly legacy for the world and our families (historically and financially).

Our mission is to:

- Motivate all to keep their dreams alive.
- Help others to understand that to achieve anything in life requires faith; belief in themselves; having a vision; working hard; having dedication and determination.
- Inspire others not to give up or lose hope. Just when we are ready to quit, our breakthrough could be right there!! So, don't quit—just persist!!
- Assure others that the possibilities are endless if we decide to act versus react.

View at: http://www.paulasmithbroadnax.com/legacy-creations/

Sign up to receive our Newsletter, updates and Events.

Paula Smith Broadnax